THE GAME BIRDS

OF

INDIA AND ASIA

THE GAME BIRDS

OF

INDIA AND ASIA

FRANK FINN, B. A. F. Z. S.

GYAN

Published by

Gyan Publishing House
5, Ansari Road
Daryaganj, New Delhi-110002
Phone: 011-47034999, 9811692060
E-mail: books@gyanbooks.com

Distribution Network
gyanbooks.com
India, USA, Canada, UK, Australia, France

ISBN: 978-81-212-8654-1 (PB)
First Published, 1911

2nd Impression 2023

Printed at: Gyan Press, Delhi.

THE GAME BIRDS OF INDIA AND ASIA
Author: FRANK FINN

Copyright. L. Medland.

PEACOCK PHEASANTS.

THE GAME BIRDS

OF

INDIA AND ASIA

BY

FRANK FINN, B.A., F.Z.S

Late Deputy Superintendent, Indian Museum

AUTHOR OF

"The Waterfowl of India and Asia," "How to know the Indian Waders," "Garden and Aviary Birds of India," "Fancy Pheasants," &c., &c

CALCUTTA: THACKER, SPINK & Co

1911

PREFACE.

THIS little work is mainly a reprint of a series of articles contributed by me some years back to the *Indian Forester*, revised and brought up to date, and with the addition of a chapter on the Sand-grouse. The Bustards I have already dealt with in my work "How to know the Indian Waders," as they are most nearly allied to certain wading birds.

The present work contains, in addition to accounts of the Game-birds of our Indian Empire, brief descriptions of the species belonging to Asia outside Indian limits, and to the East Indian islands which belong to Asia zoologically considered.

It is hoped that the usefulness of the work will thereby be increased, while any perplexity to students of the Indian and Burmese birds alone may be avoided by observing that the descriptions of all these exotic forms are in small print, while their names in the table of contents are in italics.

The scientific nomenclature employed is that of the *Fauna of British India* volumes for Indian and

Burmese species; exotic ones are to be found under the *British Museum Catalogue* names, and in the case of birds described since the publication of that work, under the names given by their describers, with references to the publication where the descriptions appeared.

I have not, however, considered it necessary to deal with the many so-called species of *Phasianus* (typical pheasants) or *Gennæus* (kaleeges) described of late years, as there is so much doubt about the validity of these, and such sub-divisions are not of any great interest to sportsmen, for whom this work is primarily designed.

F. FINN.

LONDON, 1911.

TABLE OF CONTENTS.

CHAPTER I.

CHAPTER V.

CHAPTER VI.

CHAPTER VII.

CHAPTER VIII.

PAGE.

CHAPTER IX.

CHAPTER X.

CHAPTER XI.

APPENDIX I.

APPENDIX II.

THE GAME BIRDS

OF

INDIA AND ASIA.

CHAPTER I.

INTRODUCTION.

TAKEN as a whole, no family of birds is of such general utility to mankind as the *Phasianidæ*, belonging to the order of game-birds, the *Gallinæ* (hens) or *Rasores* (scratchers) of scientists. No less than four species—the fowl, guinea-fowl, turkey and peacock—are domesticated in the full sense of the word, while several species of pheasants are reared artificially for sport or as ornamental birds. In India these birds are of special importance; the country contains an unusual variety of species and genera, and the sport they at present yield could be much improved by better protection given to the birds. For none need assistance in the struggle for existence more than game-birds do; other animals appreciate their flesh as well as man, and their general habit of breeding on the ground renders them peculiarly liable to fall a prey to terrestrial vermin Moreover, their limited powers of flight render it impossible for them to range far and wide in times of famine, and hence they are liable to perish from want, just as beasts do. On the other hand, their speed of foot and habit of frequenting cover secures them to a great extent against birds of prey; and their resident and granivorous habits render it easy for man to encourage them to any extent by means of artificial feeding. Thus, on the whole, they are easy birds to cultivate, and the encouragement of a good stock should be one of the studies of every forest officer. For not only are the birds useful for food and as affording a healthy recreation, but they are of service in a forest by destroying many noxious insects and by turning over the leaves and surface-soil in their search for these and other food. In addition to insects, some will eat mice and young snakes, so that they are good general vermin-destroyers; and though they devour much seed and grain, their own utility as food secures their being kept from increasing to such an extent as to be a pest themselves.

There is another aspect from which game birds are worthy of attention from a utilitarian point of view. They carry, as a family, far the most beautiful plumage of any group of birds; I speak after examining many specimens, dead and alive, of the long-celebrated Birds of Paradise. Not only the peacocks but several of the pheasants far excel all of these both in general brilliancy and in the individual plumes which go to make up their splendour; while the tiny humming-birds and sun-birds can never enter into competition with such large species as are the pheasants and their kin. Now, as humanity has always been constant to feathers as a means of decoration, it seems to me that the systematic cultivation of the more brilliant game birds as plume-producers would pay very well; such cultivation is well known to be profitable in the case of the ostrich, though here it entails much trouble and expense, to say nothing of positive danger from the powerful males.

Better than all, in my own private opinion, is the importance of game-birds as an adjunct to scenery. Although less imposing than the birds of flight, the graceful form and conspicuous size and colours of many of the larger species make them some of the best of ornamental birds; indeed, the peacock is the oldest "fancy" bird known, and is still admired where the cultivation of domestic monstrosities has not corrupted public taste. And if it has been worth while for humanity, for so many centuries, to foster a bird which admittedly has many faults, for its beauty alone, we may surely plead for an extension of protection to all our finest species, even if they had not solid qualities to recommend them.

Having said this much in attempted justification of game-birds as a subject for study by the most practically-minded, I may proceed to the characteristics of the family, all of which may be easily verified on the first chicken that comes to hand.

The head is notably small for the size of the bird, with a small beak, short and stout, with the upper profile arched; the nostrils are roofed over on the inner side by a gristly scale; the mouth is wide, running back nearly below the front of the eye (*N. B.*—The beak is to be measured from this point, called the *gape*, to the tip). The neck is long and the body stout and heavy; the wings are short, concave, and rounded, the pinion-quills or flight-feathers not projecting noticeably in repose in any species; the legs are powerful, the shanks stout and generally covered in front with a double row of large scales meeting in a zig-zig seam; the toes are four in number, three spreading ones in front, united at the base by a short web, and a much smaller one behind, set on at a higher level than the rest. The tail varies very much; in the fowl and many other species it is vertically folded in repose, but it is often flat like any ordinary bird's.

Internally, the birds of this family are noteworthy for their large crop or food-receptacle in the gullet, and powerful gizzard or grinding-stomach; their breast-bone is also remarkable, being so deeply cut into at each side by two great notches that hardly any of the body of the bone is left, and it presents, when cleaned, the appearance of a narrow central portion bearing the deep keel, and a somewhat V-shaped projection on each side.

The *Phasianidæ* are as uniform in their habits as in their structure, the common fowl being a fair type of all. They are, however, not all polygamous like him, nor do they all roost on a perch in the same way. Neither are all of them provided with spurs—a weapon, by the way, confined to this family. But all feed on almost anything they can get—seeds, green-food or small animal life; all trust to their legs before their wings, and fly violently rather than strongly, generally with alternate flappings and sailings; and all rigorously avoid bathing, choosing instead to roll in sand or dust to rid themselves of dirt and vermin. They are very endurant of cold, three out of the four domestic species coming from hot climates, and yet bearing the English winter well; but those which inhabit temperate regions are generally very intolerant of heat. Our hill pheasants, for instance, can ill bear the hot weather in the plains. All the species usually nest on the ground and lay several eggs.

The young of these birds, as everyone knows, can run soon after birth; they are clothed in soft down marked with brown and buff stripes. They are able to fly in a few days, and in their first feathering they most resemble the old hen, but may be known by their pointed quills. So, if none but cocks showing the full feathering are shot, one is sure of plenty of hens and young cocks to carry on the breed, and thus any number of males may be secured for food or feathers with no deterioration to the stock, but rather to its advantage; for in these so often polygamous birds a large proportion of males is a distinct disadvantage for breeding, as one is often sufficient for several females, and a larger number means much domestic discord.

It is a great help to the beginner in ornithology that the general or groups of species in the game-birds are so well defined, as will be seen later on. Some of them are, indeed, recognised by popular names:—thus, we speak of the "peafowl" and "jungle-fowl" for the species of *Pavo* and *Gallus* respectively. But under the general names of pheasants, partridges, and quails, several very distinct genera are classed in each case. However, it seems best in a work intended for beginners to maintain these popular distinctions, if only for the sake of convenience.

To commence, then, with the most familiar birds of all :—The *jungle-fowl* are distinguished by their combs, fleshy ridges of skin running from the base of the beak up the forehead : these are very small in the hens, but always discernible, and at once mark off all our three species of jungle-fowl.

The *peafowl* are at once separable by their crest and great size ; the shank is five inches long or over, none of the other members of the family having it as much as five inches. The cock Argus comes nearest, but he has a very different tail and no crest.

The *quails*, on the contrary, are very little creatures, the largest quail having a closed wing of under five inches, whereas all birds with a wing over this length may be reckoned as partridges, it being understood that the term merely refers to size.

The real difficulty lies in separating the partridges and pheasants, which make up the bulk of the family.

Pheasants are generally large birds (never under eighteen inches long), with the tail as long as the wing or longer ; when it is shorter, the difference is not more than two inches, and it only reaches this in the Tragopans and Monauls.

Partridges are almost always much smaller than pheasants, with proportionately much shorter tails ; two partridges, the snow-cocks, are bigger than many pheasants, but they have the true partridge short tail, about three inches less than the wing.

The smallest members of this family have the widest distribution, partridges and quails being found almost everywhere, the latter being especially widely spread. The pheasants, except where artificially introduced, do not occur outside of the continent of Asia as a rule, one species only, the common or Colchian pheasant, occurring in Europe. The peafowl and jungle-fowl are confined to the warm regions of South-Eastern Asia. Africa is held by the guinea-fowls, and North and Central America by the turkeys.

The boundaries between the different species and genera are settled by the right of the strongest; at any rate, in England it has been found impossible to have guinea-fowls, or golden or silver pheasants, wild along with common pheasants, since the last are not able to hold their own with these birds. When two closely-allied species of *Phasianidæ* meet, they interbreed and fuse, and what with this hybridism, and the tendency of some species to throw off sports, or "aberrations," as students of butterflies would call them, the family is a remarkably interesting one, as it undoubtedly shows better than any other some of the methods of evolution still actively in progress.

CHAPTER II.

Peafowl and Jungle-Fowl.

As these two genera are so well known and so easily recognised, it is just as well to begin with them, although they have no special relationship to each other beyond belonging to the same family. But it is always best to proceed to the unknown from the known, and a consideration of the generic and specific characters of these familiar birds will prepare us for the study of the other groups of the family.

In the case of the birds now under consideration the characters of the genera are particularly well marked and recognisable. To take the peafowl first. By "peafowl" we understand birds having the general characteristics of the Pheasant family as described above, with the addition of certain peculiarities of their own—large size, small-crested heads with bare faces, long necks and legs, and, in the males, the upper tail coverts, or feathers of the lower part of the back, of a loose filamentous texture and of enormous length, reaching several feet beyond the tail itself, which is of quite ordinary structure. The males are spurred, and sometimes the females also.

Peafowl are polygamous in their habits, several females associating with one male, who displays himself to them by "spreading out his tail," *i.e.*, erecting and spreading his upper tail-coverts with the tail braced up behind. But this gesture is common to hens and young birds also under any excitement, and it is very doubtful whether the peacock knows what he looks like, in spite of his age-long reputation for pride. And, although peahens are known to display marked preference for particular cocks, it has never been proved that they choose the most beautiful. So there is a great deal to be made out even about these familiar birds.

Peafowls are lovers of trees, on which they roost at night, and, like many game-birds, prefer to be near water. Their flight looks less laboured than that of other birds of this tribe, as their large wings flap comparatively slowly, but they cannot sustain a lengthened flight, and may even in some cases be run down. But they are very strong on their legs, and run remarkably well. They have the reputation of affecting the vicinity of tigers, and it would be interesting to know the reason of this. It is impossible that the same locality suits both creatures, and that the birds, from their very fear of the tiger, are led to keep near him in order to be informed of his movements, which certainly interest them, as they are always very wary birds.

The note of the common peacock has always been cast up to him as a defect, but it is really not an unpleasant call when heard far enough off; and it has evidently given him his name in several languages, the Greek *Taos*, French *Paon*, German *Pfau*, Dutch *Paauw* and Hindi *Mor*, all distinctly recalling the well-known note. Another point against these birds is their destructiveness in gardens; but against this may be set the great virtue that the peacock is well known to destroy small snakes, even of poisonous species. Moreover, peachicks are excellent for food, although the old birds are too tough for anything but making soup of. The genus *Pavo* is only found in South-east Asia, and comprises two species, of which by far the best known is our familiar Indian bird.

The Common or Indian Peacock.

Pavo cristatus, Fauna Brit. India, Birds, Vol. IV, p. 68.

NATIVE NAMES :—*Mor, Manjur,* Hind.; *Taus*, P. *Landuri* (the female), Mahratta *Manja* (the male), *Mania* (the female), Uriya; *Mabja*, Bhotanese; *Mong-yung*, Lepcha; *Moir*, Assamese; *Dode*, Garo; *Myl*, Tamul; *Nimili*, Telugu; *Nowl*, Canarese; *Monara*, Cingalese.

In this species of peafowl both sexes possess a crest formed of feathers webbed only at the tips, so that each is like a little fan with a long handle; moreover the bare skin of the face is white, and the female's plumage is altogether different from the male's, even allowing for the absence of the train.

The cock's head and neck are of a lovely rich greenish blue; his upper back golden green with black edgings, making the feathers look like scales; the train, or long tail-coverts, green changing to copper-red, with blue-and-purple eye-like spots: the real tail is brown, and the wings are pale dun or creamy buff with irregular black bars, except the pinion-quills which are bright chestnut, and the nearest secondary quills which are black. The under-

Copyright. L. Medland.

COMMON PEAFOWL, COCK IN MOULT, AND HEN OF THE BLACK-WINGED VARIETY.

parts are black with a green gloss, except the thighs, which are light drab.

The hen has a chestnut head and white throat. Her general colour is drab, with the quills and tail darker, and the lower part of the breast buffy white; the neck has a strong green gloss, as has also the tip of the crest.

Young cocks are at first like hens, but have a certain amount of black pencilling; their chestnut quills will also distinguish them at once. They are three years in coming into full colour.

Both sexes have dark eyes and dark horn-colour bills and feet. A fine cock may measure more than seven feet to the end of his train; the real tail is twenty inches in length only; and the closed wing about two inches less. The shank will be about five and three-quarter inches long, and the bill nearly two from the gape.

The hen is a little over a yard long, and has a proportionately shorter true tail, this being only thirteen inches, and the closed wing sixteen; the shank about five only.

This is *the* peacock *par excellence*, for although confined as a wild bird to India and Ceylon, it has been domesticated for many centuries, and is known all over the civilised world.

It does not ascend the Himalayas, as a rule, over 2,000 feet, though it may range above 5,000 on the Nilgiris; which makes it somewhat remarkable that it can bear the English climate in winter without protection.

In many places it is held sacred and found in a semi-domesticated condition, this being the case in Sind, Guzerat, Cutch and Rajputana. In any case, it is to be hoped that this magnificent bird will be spared as much as possible by sportsmen everywhere, since for its peculiar beauty it has no rival, save the even more magnificent bird next to be described.

Peafowl are not so quarrelsome as most of this family, for several cocks will show off together ; the hens usually lay, in the rains, about half-a-dozen eggs, of some shade of buff, and nearly three inches long. The nest is of course usually on the ground, but has been met with in elevated situations, and it is worth knowing that the eggs are delicious eating.

Buff varieties of this peacock have been met with in the wild state, and in domestication it is sometimes white or pied, and at times produces a most remarkable variety, the Japan or black-winged peacock (*Pavo nigripennis* of Sclater). In this form the cock's wings and thighs are black, the former being glossed with blue and green ; the pinion-quills remain chestnut. The hen of the variety is white, grizzled and splashed above with black, with a black tail, and with chestnut pinion-quills like the cock. The legs in both sexes are dirty white, not dark as in the normal form. The variety is distinct from the egg, the chicks being white, though the young cocks soon show dark feathers. Were it not known definitely to originate, in either sex, as a "sport" from the ordinary tame peafowl, this variety would certainly be ranked as a good species, since as a general rule it breeds true, and even when smaller and weaker, has been known ultimately to swamp the

Photo Copyright. L. Medland.

BURMESE PEAFOWL, HEN.

original type when all breed indiscriminately together in domestication.

The Green Peacock.

Pavo muticus, Faun. Brit. Ind., Birds, Vol. IV, p. 70.

NATIVE NAMES :—*Daung, Udaung*, Burmese; *Marait*, Talain; *Tusia*, Karen; *Burong merak*, Malay.

In this species the hen, except for the absence of the train, closely resembles the cock; the crest in both sexes is longer than in the common peafowl, and composed of feathers webbed all the way down, but gradually broadening from the root upwards, and with rounded tips; the bare face also is blue above and yellow below; moreover, the present bird is a little larger.

The cock's plumage bears a general resemblance to that of the common peacock, but differs strikingly in the neck being bronze green, the feathers having a scale-like appearance. Moreover, the wings, except the chestnut pinion-quills, are black with a blue and green gloss, and the thighs black, as in the black-winged variety of the common bird. The hen has the same bronze-green neck and dark glossy wings, but her back is dark brown, coarsely pencilled with buff, instead of green as in the cock, and the train is replaced by feathers of a more ordinary length and texture, though reaching to the end of the tail; these are golden green with irregular coarse pencilling of buff.

Young birds are like her, but show some buff edgings to the feathers. Young cocks may be distinguished from hens by having the little patch of feathers between the bill and the eye glossy green, this patch in the hen being rusty brown.

The legs and bill are blackish horn-colour, and the hen has spurs as well as the cock.

This species extends from Chittagong to Java, being the ordinary peafowl of Burma, but it is local and not abundant in most places, though it is so in some parts of Upper Burma. It has a quite different note from the ordinary peacock, this being a subdued scream in several syllables "*ayau-kau-kau-kau-kau*"; this is not at all annoying and would make the present bird a formidable rival to the other as a fancy bird were it not more delicate, and more spiteful in the case of the male. Little is known about its breeding. In captivity it has crossed with the common peafowl, the hybrid, judging from a young male in the British Museum, exhibiting a mingling of the colours of the parents, but in its crest following the common species exclusively.

The jungle-fowls are birds of a very different type, and also stand much alone, although they have an obvious affinity to the ruffed pheasants, to be mentioned later. Their characteristic points are the comb, large in the cocks and small in the hens, and the vertically folded tail, the undersides of the feathers facing each other. These characteristics apply to both sexes; the cocks alone, however, have the two central tail-feathers long and curved, and are furnished with long and sharp spurs, besides differing altogether from the hens in colour. Jungle fowls, except that they carry their tails low, much resemble tame fowls of rather small size, and are thus very easily recognisable; the various species are very distinct from each other, and only four in number: three of them occur in Indian limits.

The jungle-fowls are fond of cover, and roost on trees at night, a habit which the tame fowl has retained. His habit of crowing at night is, however, an original invention on his part, for which mankind used once to thank him, but now, alas! legally indict as a nuisance.

Jungle-fowls are often found in pairs, though a cock naturally likes to have a harem if possible, and they are very hard fighters. The cocks show off by slanting themselves over to one side, as is constantly seen in the tame fowl.

The Red Jungle-Fowl.

Gallus ferrugineus, Faun. Brit. India, Birds, Vol. IV, p. 75.

NATIVE NAMES:—*Jangal-murgh* (cock), *Jangli-murghi* (hen), Hindi; *Ban murghi*, Hindi; *Kukar*, *Kukra*, *Bankukar*, Beng.; *Ganja* (cock), Uriya; *Pazok-tohi*, *Tang-kling*, Lepcha; *Nag-tse-ja*, Bhotanese; *Bir-sim*, Kol; *Gera gogor* (cock), *Kuru* (hen), Gond; *Taukyet*, Burmese.; *Kura*, Chittagong.

In this the best known species and the ancestor of all our tame poultry, the face is naked in both sexes, though less in the hen than the cock, and there is a flap of skin below the ear—the "ear-lobe" of poultry-fanciers. The wattles, fleshy flaps of skin on each side of the throat, are usually wanting in the hen, whose comb is also very small. Even in the cock the comb, which is of the notched "single" type so familiar in tame fowls, is not so large a one as is carried by these latter.

The cock's plumage is black below and orange and red above, the neck and rump being covered by long, loose-textured feathers called "hackles" by fanciers. The tail, which has long curving upper tail-coverts hanging along each side of it, is glossy deep green, and the wings are a fine study in the arrangement of plumage, being deep glossy red, dark metallic green, black, and chestnut, put together in a diagrammatic manner most useful to ornithological students; for the minor wing coverts, the small feathers along the front edge of the wing, are black, the median, red, the major, metallic green, forming a conspicuous bar; while the primaries or pinion-quills are dingy black with paler edges and the outer halves of the secondaries or forearm-quills are cinnamon. Thus, by getting hold of a tame cock which shows the jungle-fowl colours, and such are not at all uncommon, one may master several technicalities with great ease.

After breeding, the cock casts his long neck-hackles and tail-feathers, the neck becoming clothed with a short black feathering. It is somewhat remarkable that no such change usually takes place in the tame fowl, even in India.

The cock is well over two feet long, with a wing about nine inches and shank three inches.

The hen is brown above, the colour being produced by a very fine pencilling of black and buff; below she is a plain reddish brown. Her neck, which is covered with short hackles, is streaked with black and gold, and the side feathers of the tail are black. It is a curious fact that few tame hens are coloured exactly like this.

The hen is about seventeen inches long, with a wing just over seven and shank about two and a half inches.

Young cocks, as usual, are much like the hen at first. The comb and wattles are red, and the face reddish flesh-colour; the beak dark brown, eyes red, and legs slate-colour. The ear-lobes are usually white in Indian specimens and red in those from further east, which also tend to be redder in plumage.

This species ranges from India, through Burma and the Shan States, to Siam, Cochin China, the Malay Peninsula and many eastern islands; but its precise natural range is not quite certain, as, being the ancestor of domestic fowls, it is apt to give rise to feral or secondarily wild races, owing to the escape or intentional liberation of tame poultry. It especially frequents low elevations on hills, and likes cover near cultivation; and in such places it often interbreeds with its tame descendants.

The voice of this bird is just like that of the tame fowl, but in the case of the cock's crow the resemblance is to that of the Bantam breeds, the last note being short. It breeds from March to June, laying up to eleven pale buff eggs in a rough nest on the ground. The eggs are small, scarcely exceeding two inches in length.

The red jungle-fowl, in India, is practically confined to the region where the sal-tree (*Shorea robusta*) grows; so much is this the case that an isolated wood of this tree, near Panchmarhi in the Denura valley, is occupied by this species, although the gray jungle-fowl (*Gallus sonneratii*), presently to be noticed, holds all the territory roundabout. The reason for this would be a very interesting subject for inquiry, and no doubt some forest officer will be able sooner or later to afford a solution of the problem. The red jungle-fowl is a very hard fighter, and no doubt sal jungle has some special attraction which makes him keep it to himself. In a domesticated state this species is found, as everyone knows, all over the world where it can be got to live, and its endurance of cold is most remarkable considering its tropical origin.

Many breeds have, of course, been raised from it by the selection of variations in shape and colour, but India seems to possess no particular breed except the fighting Aseel and the long lanky Chittagong, the "Malay" of home fanciers. Both of these are characterised by very small combs and wattles and short glossy plumage, which in the cocks often resembles that of the wild bird, but in hens apparently never or very rarely. The Aseel, however, is short and sturdy, not lengthy in make like its relative.

With regard to the foreign breeds now being imported, I should advise any of my readers who is starting to keep such fowls, to avoid all the feather-legged and five-toed varieties, such as the Brahma, Cochin, and Dorking, such montrosities of structure sadly handicapping a fowl's usefulness. In Calcutta there can generally be obtained excellent black China fowls, the "Langshan" of the fancy at home. This is a large bird of somewhat the Cochin type but less clumsy, and with very little feathering on the legs; many imported birds, in fact, having none. This is an excellent general utility fowl, and personally I should never trouble to send home for stock while such birds can be had in the country.

The Ceylon Jungle-Fowl.

Gallus lafayettii, Faun. Brit. India, Birds, Vol. IV.

NATIVE NAMES:—*Weli kukula* (the male), *Weli kikili* (the female), Cingalese; *kala koli*, Tamils of Ceylon.

The cock of this species bears a strong general resemblance to the red jungle-cock, but is orange-red below as well as above, the breast feathers being glossy and pointed—very like hackles in fact. The secondary quills of the wing are also purple-black instead of chestnut.

The throat and most of the rump-feathers, which are not so long and hackled as in the continental bird, are glossy violet, and the tail has a purple rather than a green gloss.

The comb also in this species has a yellow patch in the middle; the face and wattles are darker and the legs are yellow instead of slate-colour.

The hen is quite as different in her way from the red jungle-fowl hen; she is of much the same partridge-brown hue above, but has no distinct hackle on the neck; her wings are boldly barred with black, and her under-parts not cinnamon but mottled black, brown and white, becoming lighter further back. Her legs are yellow like the cock's. She has no wattles, and is feathered on the face.

Young cocks are redder above and darker below than hens. The size of this species is about the same as that of the red jungle-fowl, except that the cock's tail is longer; the hen's, on the other hand, appears to be shorter in this species.

The Ceylon jungle-fowl is confined to the island "where every prospect pleases;" but the parts thereof that especially gratify the tastes of the bird are the northern jungles and the southern hills. There seems to be a good deal of variation in the breeding season and also in the number of eggs laid, which is given as from two or twelve by different authors. There is nothing noteworthy about the appearance of these eggs.

The crow of the Ceylon cock is very different from that of the rival chanticleer of India, being two-syllabled and commonly rendered as a call to one "George Joyce." A Ceylon planter, however, told me recently that the general opinion nowadays was that the bird's friend's name was "John."

The cock is a gentleman of somewhat Don Juan-like instincts, and apt to intrude on the domestic happiness of village roosters, without the excuse that the red jungle-fowl can offer of community of descent.

The Grey or Madras Jungle-Fowl.

Gallus sonnerati, Faun. Brit. India, Birds, Vol. IV, p. 78.

NATIVE NAMES :—*Jungli murghi*, Hind.; *Komri*, Mt. Abu; *Pardah Komri*, Gondhi; *Ran-kombadi*, Mahr.; *Kathe kozhi* or *koli*, Tamil; *Adavi kode*, Telugu; *koli*, *kad koli*, Canarese.

This species also is much of the same size as the red jungle-fowl, but in the cock the tail runs very distinctly longer, and may measure as much as a foot-and-a-half long. The tail-coverts, however, are not long and curved as in the red jungle-fowl, nor are there any hackles on the rump.

The general colour of the cock is dark grey, the feathers having white shafts and grey edges, the wing-quills and tail are purple-black, and the neck feathers and those of the upper back and flat of the wing are tipped with sealing wax-like spots, orange on the wing and golden yellow on the neck. These curious tips are formed by a coalescence of the barbs of the feathers into a horny plate, and are found in a few other birds not at all allied to this family. There are rudimentary spots of the kind on the rump feathers, and a tinge of red on the flanks.

The bill is horn-colour, comb, wattles, and face red, the " ear-lobe " being indicated by a fold of skin; and the legs are usually said to be yellow, but in fine cocks they are salmon-colour. The cock moults his hackles after breeding, like the red jungle-fowl.

The hen, which has a very small comb and no wattles, is of a partridge-brown above with no distinct hackles, and white beneath with black edges to the feathers, getting narrower further back; her legs are dull faint yellow, and her comb a very dull red.

This bird, which is very striking in appearance and much admired by everyone who notices it, is confined to Southern and Western India, inhabiting hilly jungle and ranging even to the tops of the Nilgris and Pulneys. "It is found," says Blanford, "near the eastern coasts as far north as the Godavari, and in the Central Provinces its limit is some distance east of Sironcha, Chanda and Seoni. It is found throughout the Nerbudda valley west of Jubbulpore, and in parts of Central India and Rajputana, as far as the Aravalis and Mount Abu, but no farther to the northward or westward. It is met with near Baroda, but has not been observed in Kattyawar." In spite of the local intrusion of the red jungle-fowl into the grey's territory, mentioned in the account of the former species, it will be seen that on the whole their habitats are very distinct; but of course they meet occasionally. Jerdon says that near the junction of the Indravati with the Godavari he heard both species crowing within a few yards of each other, and shot one bird which was an undoubted hybrid—a remarkable fact, for hybrids between such distinct species as these are rare in nature.

The grey jungle-fowl differs very much in voice from the red bird and its poultry-yard descendant; but as authors say, the crow is very hard to describe, sounding more like a cackle, and the bird does not flap his wings before uttering it. Birds I have seen in confinement had a peculiar alarm-note when approached, sounding like "*koorchy-koorchy*," quite different from the cackle of the common fowl.

The breeding-season of this bird varies, being usually from March to July, but on the western side of the Neilgherries it is from October to December. The eggs number from seven to thirteen, and are buff-coloured and laid as usual on the ground with sometimes a few dry leaves below.

On account of its beautiful and distinct appearance, the sport it affords—for it is a wary bird—and the value of its feathers, this would be a good species to acclimatise outside India wherever there is a warm dry climate. Thus it would be excellently suited for turning out at the Cape, or in Australia or California; such extension of the habitat of a desirable bird where it does not interfere with another equally desirable, being in my opinion really justifiable acclimatisation.

The Green Jungle-Fowl.

Gallus varius, Brit. Mus. Cat., Birds, Vol. XXII, p. 352.

This beautiful bird is mostly black, with an orange patch on the wing, and a ruff of round-tipped bronze-green feathers instead of the nsual neck hackle. He has no ear-lobe or wattles, but an expansible dewlap rather like a turkey's, and his comb is not notched. It and the dewlap are most exquisitely coloured with puce and pale blue, with a yellow patch on the throat; and the face is flesh-colour, often flushing to scarlet. The hen has no comb or wattles, and is barred with black and brown, the black being much more in evidence than in the hens of other jungle-fowl. This species is found in the Malayan Islands from Java to Flores; the crow of the cock is a shrill shriek in three syllables, very like the cry of the gold pheasant in tone.

CHAPTER III.

Tragopans, Monauls, Etc.

WE now come to the large and often long-tailed game birds, commonly known as pheasants, to which may be referred eleven genera, containing more than a score of species between them. To distinguish the cocks is quite easy, but the hens, being dull-coloured, are less readily recognised, though anyone who will observe carefully enough will be able to refer any hen pheasant to her proper group also, as there are always some points she shares with her mate.

In three genera the tail is *short* in both sexes, not being longer than the wing even in the cocks, and being shorter in the hens. In this respect they approach the partridges, but they are never less than about eighteen inches long, which is much bigger than any partridge except the great Ramchukors or snow-cocks. And in these there is a difference of three inches between the length of the wing and tail; whereas in these short-tailed pheasants the wing never exceeds the tail by so much as this.

These genera are the Tragopans, Monauls, and Blood-Pheasants, which are easily distinguished from any others of the family.

The *Blood-Pheasant* is only about eighteen inches long, with very long, soft plumage and bright red legs.

The *Monauls* (two species) are large birds, two feet long or more, with unusually large bills for game-birds, and short legs; the bill from gape to tip is about two-thirds the length of the shank.

The *Tragopans* (three species) are also large, about two feet long; but their bills are remarkably small, and their legs rather long, the bill being less than half the length of the shank.

In five genera the tail is distinctly longer than the wing, even in the hen, and very long indeed in the cock, this being the typical pheasant shape of tail, with the centre feathers much the longest. These groups are easily made out.

The *Argus* has a bare head and the primary quills distinctly shorter than the secondaries, which more than cover them.

The *Peacock Pheasant* has a long broad tail with rounded tips to the feathers.

The *Typical Pheasants* (two species) have long tails with pointed tips to the feathers; the males have a bare red skin round the eye.

The *Cheer Pheasant* has a very long-pointed tail and a crest, with a red skin round the eye in both sexes.

The *Amherst Pheasant* has a long-pointed tail and a pale blue or green skin round the eye in both sexes, with a ruff in the male.

There remains three genera with tails of *medium* length, taking males and females together; the tail being about as long as the wing or shorter in the latter, and rather longer in the former, though never so extravagantly long as in the last group.

The tail is, even in the short-tailed hens, much graduated, with the outside pair of feathers only half as long as the middle ones, which is not the case in the short-tailed pheasants alluded to above, whose tails are merely rounded. Of this section :—

The *Koklass Pheasants* (two species) are distinguished by having the face feathered all over, and most of their feathers pointed-tipped.

The *Fire-back* has, in both sexes, a short folded tail, much like a common hen's, and a bare bright blue face.

The *Kaleeges* (about half-a-dozen species) have crests in both sexes, and also a bare red face, with tails long or short, folded like a fowl's. The exact number of species in this group is uncertain, and the length of the tail varies in the cocks, but as a whole they are very recognisable.

To discuss the short-tailed genera first: the Tragopans, in addition to their large size, small bills, and rounded shortish tails, are notable for their long, slender toes and intricately mottled plumage. The tail is carried low, and is inclined to fold.

In the cocks the plumage is always more or less mixed with red and speckled with light spots; they also have a full crest, and fleshy horns and a dewlap, most developed in the breeding-season, and expansible. The dewlap at most times is a mere fold of skin along the throat, and the horns lie concealed in the crest. But when the bird faces the female to show off, the horns elongate themselves and the dewlap comes down and spreads out into a bib or apron, showing the most brilliant colours. The cock also shows off by slanting himself over, like a common fowl.

In most male birds of this genus the face is bare, and they are provided with spurs. The colouration of this sex is very complicated and beautiful, but it is not necessary to describe it fully, as the different species are readily recognisable. The hens have no fleshy appendages or crest, and are feathered up to the eyes; they have shorter tails than the cocks, and no spurs. Their plumage is a very intricate pepper-and-salt mixture, a great deal easier to recognise than to describe.

Tragopans inhabit hill forest at a high elevation, and are great skulkers, avoiding observation as much as possible. They spend a great deal of their time in trees, feeding on leaves and berries to a very large extent.

The note of the cock Tragopans is most remarkable, being compared to a bleat or a bellow rather than a crow, but they are silent birds, as a rule, except in the breeding season. They are not easy to shoot, and sometimes rather poor eating, but for their peculiar beauty of plumage they are unrivalled. Only five species are known, all Indian or Chinese. Our birds are often called Argus Pheasants, but the real Argus is a very different bird, as will be shown later.

The Crimson Tragopan.

Tragopan satyra, Faun. Brit. Ind., Birds, Vol. IV, p. 99.

NATIVE NAMES :—*Lungi*, Hind. in Garhwal and Kumaun; *Monal* in Nepal; *Omo*, *Bap*, Bhutia; *Tar-rhyak*, Lepcha.

In this species the male's face and throat are thinly feathered; the general plumage is rich red on the neck and below, and mottled black and brown above, sprinkled nearly all over with round white spots edged with black; the head and tail are black, with a red band round the back of the former; the bend of the wing is also red, and there are red patches on the mottled brown plumage of the rest of the wing and the rump.

The bill is blackish brown, the horns sky-blue, and the skin of the face and the throat rich deep blue, the bib being blue, with large red lateral spots when expanded; the eyes are dark and the legs flesh-coloured.

The hen is of a rich brown, paler below, grizzled and mixed with black and buff. Her beak is dark horn-colour, and her legs fleshy grey.

Young birds are like the hen, but distinctly streaked with buff; young cocks assume male plumage very gradually.

The male is well over two feet long, with wing and tail each about ten inches, and shank over three, and twice as long as the bill. The hen is under two feet, with the tail shorter than the wing.

This species, one of the most richly-coloured birds in existence, inhabits the Himalayas from Garhwal to Bhootan, ranging according to season from six to twelve thousand feet in elevation. It breeds in May, laying eggs much like large hen's eggs, white with pale dull lilac markings, and about two and-a-half inches long.

The Black or Western Tragopan.

Tragopan melanocephalus, Faun. Brit. Ind., Birds, Vol. IV, p. 101.

NATIVE NAMES :—*Jewar, Jowar*, in Garhwal; *Jaighi, Jajhi*, Bashahr; *Sing-monal*, Hindi in N.-W. Himalayas; *Jigurana* (the cock), *Budal* (the hen), Kulu, Mandi and Suket; *Falgur*, Chamba.

This bird has a longer crest than the Crimson Tragopan, and is a little larger, with a slightly shorter tail; the face of the cock is also bare. His prevailing colour is black, grizzled with buff above, and spotted with white both there and below. The neck is red, brightest in front; and the top of the crest and bend of the wing are also red; there is also a certain admixture of red below the breast. The bill is blackish, eyes brown, legs flesh-coloured, and horns blue as usual; but the bare face is bright red, and the dewlap purple in the middle, and showing spots of blue and flesh-colour at the sides.

The hen is of a grizzled brown, much greyer in tone than that of the Crimson Tragopan hen, and with the pale spots below—which are white, not buff—better defined and dark-bordered. Her feet are grey.

This bird inhabits the North-Western Himalayas from Garhwal to Hazara. It nowhere meets the crimson species, their respective limits being separated by a distance of about four days' march. It keeps near the snow in summer, descending lower in winter. The eggs, six in number, of a pale buff minutely freckled, were taken in Hazara in May by Captain Lautour. They seem to be slightly smaller than those of the red species.

The Grey-breasted or Assam Tragopan.

Tragopan blythii, Faun. Brit. Ind., Birds, Vol. IV, p. 102.

NATIVE NAMES :—*Hur-huria*, *Sansaria*, Assam; *Gnu*, Angami Naga; *Chingtho*, Kuki.

This is smaller than the other Indian species, and has a shorter crest and tail. The male has a black head, with red eye-brows meeting behind, the neck and bend of the wing red as usual, and the underparts below the breast smoky grey; the upper plumage is black mottled with buff and spotted with white and red; the tail is black. The bare face and throat are yellow, running into green below; the bill and eyes dark, the horns blue, and the feet flesh-coloured as in other male Tragopans.

The hen is of the usual hen Tragopan grizzle, less grey in tone than the black Tragopan hen; from the hen of the crimson species she may be distinguished by having a greater proportion of black above, and being mottled with dirty cream-colour instead of buff below, the upper and under surface being thus more strongly contrasted than in the other. These hen Tragopans are easy enough to distinguish on comparison, but as no two species inhabit the same tract, this will rarely be necessary.

Copyright. L. Medland.

TEMMINCK'S TRAGOPAN, COCK.

Copyright. L. Medland

AMHERST PHEASANT, COCK.

The present species inhabits Manipur and the Naga Hills south of Assam, ranging from five to ten thousand feet according to season, like the other species. It has also been known to occur in the Dafla Hills north of Assam. It feeds chiefly on berries and affects high oak forest. Its breeding in the wild state is not known, but an egg laid in confinement was buff finely speckled with reddish brown. I have seen in the London Zoo a hybrid cock, bred between this species and the *T. temminckii* mentioned below. It hardly showed the cross at all, almost precisely resembling a pure *T. blythii*, and having the same yellow and green throat, but the grey under-parts were variegated with red.

The Grey-Spotted or Temminck's Tragopan.

Tragopan temmincki, Brit. Mus. Cat., Birds, Vol. XXII, p. 275.

This may be distinguished from the crimson Tragopan, which it much resembles, by having the light spots on the plumage larger, grey instead of white, and without the black borders; the face is also bare of feathers, the hens of the two species are alike. This Tragopan is found in South China, and has been obtained in our territory near Sodon.

The Buff or Cabot's Tragopan.

Tragopan caboti, Brit. Mus. Cat., Birds, Vol. XXII, p. 277.

The male of the buff Tragopan is entirely plain buff below, and is spotted with buff above on a ground of mottled red and black; the bare face is scarlet, with blue eyebrows. The hen

may be distinguished from that of the crimson Tragopan, which she much resembles, by her smaller size. This species is also Chinese. The eggs, buff, thickly speckled, with pale-brown, and four in number, have been taken from an old squirrel's nest 30 feet up in a tree, and in captivity this species has also nested in an old nest in a tree.

The Monauls are very easily recognisable birds, being of large size and stout and heavy make, with comparatively large heads and bills, short shanks—shorter than the middle toe, and tails of only medium length, flat and nearly square like a pigeon's. There is a bare blue space round the eye in both sexes, but in plumage they differ absolutely, and the cocks only possess spurs, which are not very long. Four species are known, of which two are Indian.

The Common Monaul or Impeyan Pheasant.

Lophophorus refulgens, Faun. Brit. Ind., Birds, Vol. IV, p. 96.

NATIVE NAMES :—*Lont* (male), *Hani* (female), *Nil-mor*, *yung-limor*, Kashmir ; *Nilgur*, Chamba ; *Munal*, *Nil* (male), *Karari* (female), Kulu ; *Munál*, *Ghar-Munál*, *Ratia Kawan*, *Rabnal*, *Ratkap*, N.-W. Himalayas ; *Datiya*, Kumaun and Garhwal ; *Dafia*, Nepalese ; *Fo-dong*, Lepcha ; *Cham-dong*, Bhutias of Sikkim.

The male Monaul has a fine crest of feathers with shafts bare nearly to the tip, where there is a lance-head-shaped webbed portion ; it is more or less erect. This crest and the head generally and a streak along each side of the breast are of an intensely brilliant burnished-green ; the back of the neck is burnished copper-red, changing to golden-green in some lights; the upper part of the back is bronze-green, the lower silver-white. This latter colour is usually concealed by the wings, which are metallic purple with metallic blue tips to the feathers. The under-surface of the body is velvety black, and the tail cinnamon.

The hen has a short crest of ordinary feathers; she is of a mottled-brown, the light marking tending to run in streaks. Her throat is pure white, and her general appearance is much like that of a huge partridge.

The young birds resemble her; the young male, however, has a buff patch on the back where the white one is found in the adult: he does not attain his full plumage till the second year, and even then, curiously enough, the seventh pinion-quill remains brown for a year more.

The beak of the Monaul is horn-colour and the legs olive-green—what is called "willow" by poultry fanciers. The bright blue face noted above is most characteristic of these birds. The cock is about twenty-eight inches long, with the wing nearly a foot and the tail nine and a half, the shank three inches in length and the bill two. The hen is a little over two feet long.

The common Monaul is found throughout the Himalayas, and even extends west to Afghanistan and Chitral. It varies its vertical range according to the time of year and the part of the hills inhabited, going higher in the Eastern Himalayas than the Western, and of course much higher in summer than in winter. It is not likely to be found, however, above 15,000 or below 4,500 feet at any time.

It is usually a forest bird, although in summer it may be found out on the grassy slopes above the level of trees. Only a few are seen in company, males being more solitary than females. The food is especially composed of grubs and roots, the Monaul being much addicted to digging, an operation it performs with its beak, for it does not scratch like most birds of this family. The comparatively large bill, however, forms a most effective hoe, and the bird is probably of great use in the forest in turning over the surface and destroying insect pests..

It is likewise most excellent eating, and carries a great deal of meat, so that it is in every way a bird to be encouraged.

The Monaul breeds in May and June, the hen laying sometimes as many as six eggs, but generally fewer, in a nest under a bush or tuft of grass. The eggs are buff, speckled with brown, like turkey's eggs. The display of the cock is of the frontal type, the attitude being much like that of the turkey. His call is a loud plaintive whistle, unlike the harsh notes of most birds of this family; and the hen's note is similar.

It is worth knowing, considering how many people now reside in the hills for long periods, that the Monaul is capable of complete domestication; the birds may be brought up so tame that they can be allowed to go about at large like poultry. The species is also a very suitable one for acclimatisation as a game bird wherever congenial localities exist, as it affords good sport, being wary and readily taking wing. The cock varies a good deal in colour, black, white and pied varieties, and others with the copper on the neck replaced by steel-blue having been recorded. The last-named has been described as a distinct species under the name of *Lophophorus mantoui*.

The Bronze-backed Monaul.

Lophophorus impeyanus, Faun. Brit. Ind., Birds, Vol. IV, p. 97.

The male of this species resembles the last in size and form, but differs in having the lower back bronze and purple instead of white, and the underparts glossed with green instead of being jet black. The hen is not known, and only a very few of the other sex have been obtained, all in Chamba, south-east of Kashmir.

It seems, from an account by Major G. S. Rodon, in the Journal of the Bombay Natural History Society, that the native *shikaries* of the locality say that this form is merely a "sport" from the common Monaul, which likewise occurs there. Considering the proneness of the common species to variation, and the unlikelihood of two species of pheasants, differing only in colour, remaining distinct in the same district, I am strongly inclined to think that their account is correct, and that the Bronze-backed Monaul, like the Black-winged Peacock, is not a true species, though excellently exemplifying a variation from which a species may arise. The subject is one which would well repay investigation, and I hope that anyone who may be living in Chamba will look out for a cock Monaul showing no white upon the back, and thenceforward investigate his family and relationships, if possible. It is a pity to kill the bird, as the form is now known, and it would be more interesting scientifically to find out about its propagation, although, of course, breeding in confinement would be an easier and simpler means to this end.

The Crestless Monaul.

Lophophorus sclateri, Brit. Mus. Cat., Birds, Vol. XXII, p. 282.

This species differs markedly from the common Monaul in having no crest, but the crown of the cock covered with short curly or frizzled feathers. The wings are also shorter. In general colour the two species are very similar, but the male of the crestless bird has the upper tail-coverts and tip of the tail white as well as the rump. In the hen the rump is very light and the tail has a broad white tip. This species inhabits the Mishmi Hills.

Lhuys's Monaul.

Lophophorus l'huysii, Brit. Mus. Cat., Birds, Vol. XXII, p. 81.

NATIVE NAMES.—*Pae-mow-ky, Ho-than-ky*, Chinese.

This is larger than the common Monaul, and has a crest of ordinary-shaped feathers. The general colour is similar to that of the common species, but with more of the copper-colour, and the tail glossy green and blue instead of cinnamon. The hen differs from the common Monaul hen in having a large white patch on the back. This species inhabits Western Szechuen and Eastern Koko-nor, and is said to be becoming very rare through persecution by the natives.

The Blood-Pheasant.

Ithagenes cruentus, Faun. Brit. Ind., Birds, Vol. IV., p. 103.

NATIVE NAMES :—*Chilimé*, Nepalese ; *Semo*, Bhutan ; *See-mong*, Lepcha.

Only one species of this very well-marked genus is found with us. It is a small bird for a pheasant, being about a foot and a half long, with a broad rounded tail not so long as the closed wing, the whole bird being thus rather partridge-like in style. The plumage is very characteristic, being long, full, and soft ; the crown has a short bushy crest, and there is bare skin round the eye. Cock and hen are much alike in shape, but differ absolutely in colour, and the former has several spurs on each leg.

In colour he is grey streaked with white above and on the flanks and lower belly ; the breast is apple-green splashed with crimson, and the throat and feathers under the tail are crimson.

The hen is brown, finely pencilled with black, and with a grey cap and chestnut throat.

The legs are coral-red, as also are the base of the bill and the bare eye-patch, which is brighter in the male, however. The bill is black.

The cock will measure about eighteen inches, with a wing of eight and-a-half, tail nearly seven, shank nearly three, and bill under one inch. The hen is a little smaller. This is a thoroughly alpine bird, ranging between ten and fourteen thousand feet in the Himalayas, where alone it is found. It occurs in Nepal, Sikkim, and Bhutan, but its exact eastern and western limits are unknown, except that it does not extend to Kumaon. In Sikkim, at all events, it inhabits pine forests, feeding on the shoots of the conifers and on various other leaves, seeds, and fruits. The flavour consequently varies, and sometimes it is so strong and unpleasant that the bird is hardly fit to eat at all.

In such cases the objectionable taste could probably be in great measure removed by "drawing" the birds as soon as killed, as no doubt the food they contain taints the meat.

The young have been seen in May, but beyond this nothing is known of the breeding of the species. Birds of the year have no spurs, and in older specimens they vary in number, being different on each leg; four on one and five on the other seems to be the maximum. With such saw-like shanks the Blood-Pheasant cock ought to be able to give a good account of himself in a fight; but in the autumn, at all events, males and females are found associating together in flocks of more than a dozen. The Blood-Pheasant is not a shy bird, and much prefers running to flying; its call note is a squeal like a kite's, while it has a shorter cry of alarm. It is suspected of burrowing under the snow in winter like some grouse; indeed, the short-tailed hill pheasants of the East recall grouse in more ways than one, and evidently take the place of those birds in the economy of nature.

Only two other species of the present genus are known :—

Geoffroy's Blood-Pheasant.

Ithagenes geoffroyi, Brit. Mus. Cat. Birds, Vol. XXII, p. 269.

The male of this species much resembles the Indian bird, but has the throat and breast grey, thus being duller in colour, while the hen is greyer above and has the tail indistinctly edged with crimson.

This Blood-Pheasant is found in Eastern Tibet and Western Szechuen, and so comes near Indian limits.

Chinese Blood-Pheasant.

Ithagenes sinensis, Brit. Mus. Cat., Birds, Vol. XXII, p. 270.

NATIVE NAME.—*Sermean*, Kan-su.

The male can be distinguished from the Indian bird by the blackish-brown sides of the crest, blackish-grey front of the neck, and by having a rusty-brown patch on the wing where there is a green one in the other two species. The hen is most like that of the Indian bird, but has a grey instead of brown throat. This species inhabits high mountains in China.

CHAPTER IV.

The Long-tailed Pheasants.

Of the various long-tailed types of pheasants, the true Argus is certainly the most remarkable, the genus being quite unique among birds in general. The most important characters, in addition to the bare head and long secondary quills mentioned in the previous chapter, are the rather long legs and the tail, which is folded like that of a common fowl and composed of only 12 feathers. It is only moderately long in the hen, barely exceeding the wing; but in the cock the middle tail feathers are of enormous length, up to over four feet. In this sex also the secondary quills, which are very broad as well as long, exceed the primaries by considerably more than a foot; even in the hen the primaries are some inches shorter than the secondaries.

The Argus.

Argusianus argus, Faun. Brit. Ind., Birds, Vol. IV, p. 71.

NATIVE NAMES :—*Quou*, *Burong quou*, *Kwang*, Malay; *Kyekwah*, Siamese at Bankasoon.

The plumage of this bird would be very difficult to describe in full, but it is not hard briefly to characterise. In both sexes it is mostly of a dark

 . Medland.

ARGUS PHEASANT, COCK.

brown, closely mottled with buff, the breast being of a plain bay; the bare head is blue, and the legs red; the cock has no spurs.

As above noted, he differs from the hen in his enormous secondary quills and central tail feathers, the latter being curiously twisted at the end. The male Argus's wing-quills, also, both primary and secondary, bear the elaborate decoration which makes him one of the most wonderful birds in the world, but none of this is visible in the ordinary attitude of repose. The primary quills have a dark blue shaft, and a band of chestnut, finely dotted with white alongside it on the inner web of the feather; the secondaries have along the shafts of their outer webs a row of most beautiful eye spots, or "ocelli," shaded with ochre, drab, and white, so beautifully as to resemble balls lying in sockets, the "lights" being most artistically rendered. As Darwin has shown, on the plumage of this bird a complete gradation can be traced from these wonderful markings to ordinary spots. Another peculiarity of the male, concealed in repose, is that the lower part of the back is buff with black spots.

The male is altogether larger than the female, and his extravagant developments of plumage make him seem even bigger than he is. He is about six feet long, with a tail of over four feet; the wing to the end of the great secondaries is nearly a yard long, but the primaries are only about a foot and a half; the shank is four and a half inches long, and the bill rather more than one and a half. In the hen the length is about two and a half feet; the wing a foot, and the tail an inch more; the shank is about an inch shorter than the male's. Her general appearance somewhat suggests both a fowl and a turkey.

In our empire this bird is only found in the extreme south of Tenasserim, but it inhabits the Malay Peninsula generally, as well as Sumatra and the Laos mountains in Siam. It is a true jungle bird, confined to evergreen forest, and hardly ever seen, as it is very wary and a great skulker. There appears to be no regular breeding season, nor do the birds associate in pairs or families. The hens wander about casually, and the males remain near clearings, which each makes for himself, picking all the weeds, leaves, etc., off an area a few yards square. In this he generally lives, roosting at night on a tree close by, and going out to feed on fallen fruit and insects.

Here, too, he is too frequently captured by various poaching devices in the way of snares and deadfalls, for there is a considerable demand for his beautiful plumage. A good many birds also seem to be taken alive: they are very quiet and easy to tame.

It is in his arena, presumably, that the cock displays himself to the hen, for he has a most remarkable and elaborate display, which requires a good deal of space. This has frequently been witnessed in captivity; and I have seen it more than once myself. The cock, when at full show, spreads his wings to their fullest extent, at the same time bringing them down in front till they meet before his head, while behind they are elevated so as almost to meet in front of the raised spread tail, the whole effect being of a great, painted, almost vertical screen or fan, hiding the head and body completely. The bird, however, which is careful to have the hen in front of him, in some cases every now and then pushes his head between two of his quills to see what effect he is producing.

The said effect, in the cases I have observed, was absolutely *nil*; but very likely a captive hen, confined always with the male, is bored and indifferent. I did not see the peeping manœuvre on his part, but traces of its frequent performance may be found in the worn quills in skins.

The Argus does not seem to fight at all, and has been observed to give up his cherished parlour to an aggressive Fire-back pheasant without a struggle; but our old bird at the Calcutta Zoological Garden would fly at a hand presented to him, striking with bill and feet. In a wild state the males answer each other's calls. The note is a very curious one for a bird, a sort of double whoop, somewhat recalling the note of the Hoolock Apes, though not so rapidly repeated as theirs. The hen has a note of several syllables, more quickly uttered, but of somewhat the same type.

She seems to lay at any time, the eggs being seven or eight in number and reddish buff in tint. Although the nest is, as usual, on the ground, the young fledge sufficiently to fly and take to a perch in a very few days.

The Argus, as it can hardly ever be *seen* wild, to say nothing of being shot, is rather out of court as a game-bird; but it has considerable value as a menagerie specimen, live birds fetching about thirty rupees each in Calcutta. It seems to me, therefore, that snaring in such a way as to cause its death should be prohibited, and its capture in any way regulated, as, if preserved, the high price it fetches would render it a profitable as well as harmless inmate of our jungles.

Gray's Argus.

Argusianus grayi, Brit. Mus. Cat., Birds, Vol. XXII, p. 365.

Only one other species of true Argus is certainly known, from Borneo, which is rather smaller than our bird, but does not differ much from it otherwise, being merely redder on the breast, with paler mottling above.

Double-spotted Argus.

Argusianus bipunctatus, Brit. Mus. Cat., Birds, Vol. XXII, p. 366.

There is in existence, however, a piece of a primary quill feather, now in the British Museum, on the evidence of which a presumed third species has been named. In this specimen the white-dotted cinnamon patch is found on *both* sides of the shaft, which is slighter than that of a corresponding quill from the common Argus. It is not known what the other feathers of this specimen were like or where it came from, and it might have been merely a "sport;" if so, it was certainly a progressive one, tending to greater ornamentation than the ordinary species possesses.

The Crested Argus.

Rheinardtius ocellatus, Brit. Mus. Cat., Vol. XXII, p. 367.

This Argus is of a different type of form from the typical Argus above described, having wings of ordinary size in both sexes, which are also provided with a large erect tuft-crest on the back of the head. The male has all the tail-feathers very long, broad and pointed.

The colouration is very complicated, being of a brown, diversified with numerous fine chestnut and white markings in the male, and black and buff pencilling in the hen, but the characteristic shape is quite distinctive. The male's tail is five feet long; that of the hen is about fourteen inches. The species is found in the Tonquin mountains; a race with darker upper parts, and lighter markings, in the males, occurring at Pahang in the Malay Peninsula, it has never, so far as I know been brought to Europe alive.

We have next to consider the Peacock-Pheasants, or *Polyplectrons*, which are rather small birds as pheasants go, with long legs, short rounded wings, and long flattish tails, composed of as many as twenty broad rounded feathers. The upper tail coverts are also very long and broad. The general build is light, and the birds are very active. There is a bare skin round the eye in both sexes; but the female is smaller and less bright than the male, and is not spurred, whereas the male has more than one spur on each leg, whence the scientific name, which means "many-spurred."

Only one species is certainly known as occurring in our empire.

The Grey Peacock-Pheasant.

Polyplectrum chinquis, Faun. Brit. Ind., Birds, Vol. IV, p. 73.

NATIVE NAMES :—*Paisa-walla majur*, Cachar Tea-Garden coolies; *Munnowur*, *Deyodahuk*, Assamese; *Deodurug*, *Deodirrik*, Garo Hills; *Kat-mor*, Chittagong; *Doun-kalah*, Arrakan and Pegu; *Shwedong*, Tenasserim.

The male of this species has a rather short, hairy-looking crest, always standing on end; his tail is several inches longer than the closed wing. The general plumage is a grizzle, produced by numberless tiny cream-coloured spots on a drab ground, but the throat is pure white, and the back, wings, and tail studded with eye-spots of green shot with purple, and bordered with cream colour.

"Studded" exactly expresses the effect, for so beautifully shaded are these spots that they seem to stand out from the feather like convex bosses of metal. They are round, small and single on the back and wings; large, oval and double on the tail and its upper coverts; in all cases being near the tip of the feather. His bill and legs are dull black, eyes white, and face pale sickly yellow.

The hen is considerably smaller than the cock, and has the tail much shorter even in proportion, this being less than two inches longer than the wing in her. In general style of plumage she resembles the male, but has a shorter crest, is duller and darker in colour, and has, instead of eye-spots, ill-defined black patches, with only a faint gloss of green. On the longest tail-feathers and their coverts, even these poor apologies for eye-spots are absent. Her bill, legs, and face are less decided in colour, and her eyes grey. The male is just over two feet long, with a fourteen-inch tail and wing of over nine inches; his shanks are three inches long, provided with from one to three spurs each; his bill about an inch and a half from corner of mouth to tip.

The hen is only nineteen inches in length, with a nine-inch tail, and wing of less than eight inches; the shank is only about a quarter of an inch shorter than her mate's.

The Peacock-Pheasant ranges from Sikkim through Assam and Burma to Siam, always keeping on or near hills, though not a bird of high elevations, as it seems not to range above six thousand feet. It frequents thick jungle on hill sides and ravines, and is very wary and hard to approach. The male has a most unpleasant call, a kind of harsh barking cackle, and will often reply to a gunshot with it. In showing off to the female he manages to display all his beauties at once, by raising one wing and lowering the other, at the same time spreading and slanting his tail, so as to exhibit all his spots on the side turned towards her. He also displays frontally crouching down with spread erected tail and wings set out on each side. In captivity he is true to one mate, and she displays an interesting method of protecting her chicks, keeping her broad tail spread horizontally as a sort of natural umbrella to hide and shelter them as they follow her. They, in their turn, have the instinct to follow closely so strongly developed that when specimens were hatched under a Bantam fowl at the London Zoological Gardens, they persisted in running close behind her. In this way they got more kicks than cover, and it was not till the Peacock-Pheasant herself hatched chicks that the habit was understood.

The eggs of the Peacock-Pheasant are buff-coloured and about two inches long; tame birds only lay two. The wild ones nest about May.

Malayan Peacock-Pheasant.

Polyplectrum bicalcaratum, Brit. Mus. Cat., Birds, Vol. XXII, p. 357.

The male of this is speckled with black instead of cream-colour, and has a longer crest, glossed with purple and green. The hen is also easily distinguishable by the dark instead of light speckling. This species inhabits the Malay Peninsula.

Germain's Peacock-Pheasant.

Polyplectrum germaini, Brit. Mus. Cat., Birds, Vol. XXII, p. 357.

This has no crest at all; its plumage is light-speckled, but darker in tone than in our grey bird, and the eye-spots on the tail feathers are longer. In the hen the eye-spots are better developed than in that of our species, and are found on the longer tail-coverts. Germain's Peacock-Pheasant is found in Cochin-China; a smaller race of species (*P. katsumatæ*) with the eye-spots greener and less purple and the mottling finer, inhabits Hainan. The males, at all events, of this and the last Peacock-Pheasant have the bare skin of the face red, so that a red-faced Peacock-Pheasant in British territory is a bird to keep one's eye upon.

Bornean Peacock-Pheasant.

Polyplectrum schleiermacheri, Brit. Mus. Cat., Birds, Vol. XXII, p. 259.

This Bornean representative of the Malayan Peacock-Pheasant chiefly differs from it by having the under parts mostly black in the male, but white down the centre, the chest being spangled with purplish-green; the hen, like the hen of the Malayan species, has eye-spots on the end of the tail-feathers, but not on the longer tail-coverts as that species' female has; and she is washed with black below.

Napoleon's Peacock-Pheasant.

Polyplectron napoleonis, Brit. Mus. Cat., Birds, Vol. XXII, p. 361.

This, the smallest and most beautiful of the Peacock-Pheasants, inhabits the island of Palawan in the Philippines. The cock, which is only about as big as the hen of the common Indian Peacock-Pheasant, has a long-pointed crest; the general colour of the plumage is black, glossed with blue and green above; the lower back and tail are buff, speckled with black, and the tail is marked with blue-and-green eye-spots. The hen which is smaller, is also crested, and has the crown black; the plumage generally is brown, mottled with black, and there are green eye-spots on the tail.

Purple-tailed-Pheasant.

Chalcurus chalcurus, Brit. Mus. Cat., Birds, Vol. XXII, p. 361.

This peculiar Sumatran Pheasant is closely allied to the Peacock-Pheasants, but has the sides of the face feathered, and the tail as long and narrow as in the typical Pheasants ; there are no eye-spots, and the general plumage of both sexes is pencilled with light and dark brown ; the tail is of a glossy purplish blue at the tip and sides.

Intermediate Peacock-Pheasant.

Chalcurus inopinatus, ROTHSCHILD, Bull. Brit. Ornith. Club, Vol. XIII, p. 41.

The close relationship of the last species with the Peacock-Pheasants is proved by the recent discovery of this intermediate form from Ulu Pahang in the Malayan Peninsula ; it has long patches instead of eye-spots on the tail, which is shaped as in *C. chalcurus*, but has eye-spots on the upper parts; the hen also bears faint editions of these.

Lady Amherst's Pheasant.

Chrysolophus amherstiæ, Brit. Mus. Cat., Birds, Vol. XXII, p. 342.

NATIVE NAME :—*Seng-ky*, Chinese.

The male of this species is a remarkable-looking bird, not to be mistaken for anything else, though the hen is not at all striking. The cock has a long narrow crest from the back of the head, a cape or ruff (which can be spread out like a fan) covering the back of the neck, and an immensely long tail, with the centre feathers particularly long and broad, and arched transversely, so as to roof over the rest. The upper tail-coverts are also very long, and lie along the sides of the tail like the "side hangers" of a cock. The bare face, of a livid blue or green, is almost the only point which this very over-dressed bird shares with the hen of his species.

If his attire were less exuberant, Lady Amherst's godchild would still attract attention by his startling colouring. His crown, throat, breast, upper back, and wings, are rich metallic dark green, with black edgings to the feathers ; the under-parts below the breast are pure white. The ruff is white, with black edgings to each feather, and the enormous centre tail-feathers are also white, with black bars and pencillings ; the side tail-feathers are brown and differently marked. The whole is set off by the blood-red crest, scarlet tips to the long upper tail-coverts, and by the lower back being yellow, bordered with scarlet where it nears the tail.

The eyes are white, and the legs bluish like the face. The length of this bird is over four feet, but a yard of this is tail ; the wing barely exceeds eight inches, and the shank three ; it is a smaller and lighter-made bird than the home pheasant.

The hen is brown, boldly barred with black, especially upon the upper surface of the body. She has a bare bluish or greenish space round the eye, and grey legs, like the cock, but her eyes are dark. Her zebra-like markings will easily distinguish her from the hen of Stone's pheasant, the only one for which she could be mistaken. Besides, her tail is much longer in proportion than that bird's, being more than a foot long, although she is a smaller bird.

This remarkable bird is one of the latest additions to the fauna of our Empire, having only been introduced to our notice in 1899 by Mr. Oates who had an opportunity of inspecting a male specimen which had been obtained by one of the officers attached to the Boundary Delimitation Commission, on the Burmo-Chinese frontier.

The proper habitat of the species is the mountains of Western China and Eastern Tibet. It was introduced into Europe alive a good many years ago, and is probably now better known as an aviary bird than in the wild state.

Golden Pheasant.

Chrysolophus pictus, Brit. Mus. Cat., Birds, Vol. XXII, p. 339.

NATIVE NAME :—*Kin-ky*, Chinese.

The cock of this species, which has long been a well-known fancy bird both in India and Europe, is chiefly golden above and scarlet below; he is ruffed and crested like the Amherst, the crest being fuller than in that bird; but his tail is not so large. The hen is extremely like the Amherst hen above described, but has dull yellow legs and no bluish bare skin round the eye. Moreover, the general tone of her plumage is yellower, and there is a wash of gold on the top of her head. The gold pheasant inhabits the mountains of South and West China, but is kept in domestication in many countries.

The Cheer Pheasant.

Catreus wallichi, Faun. Brit. Ind., Birds, Vol. IV, p. 82.

NATIVE NAMES :—*Chihir*, *Chir*, Nepal, Kumaun, Garhwal, &c.; *Bunchil*, *Herril*, N. of Mussoorie; *Chaman*, Kulu and Chamba.

The Cheer bears a close general resemblance to the typical pheasants of the genus *Phasianus*, having the same style of tail and no ruff; but the head is furnished with a long narrow-pointed crest in both sexes, which also have in common a bare red skin round the eye. This style of head is characteristic of some Kaleeges, as will be seen in the next chapter; and its combination with the long narrow true pheasant tail makes the Cheer quite unique and easily recognisable. The male Cheer is larger than the female, and is spurred; but the latter has nearly as long a tail in proportion, and is not much duller in colour, though different in pattern: the cock Cheer being an unusually dull bird for a pheasant.

His general colour is a buffy white, closely barred with black above and sparingly mottled with that colour below; his head is drab, and the front and sides of his neck plain dirty white; the lower part of his back is warm buff barred with steely black, and his tail is really handsome, being rich buff, barred with broad bands of mixed chestnut and black. The middle of the belly is black, and the flanks rusty yellow.

The bill is pale grey-brown, and the feet drab.

In length the cock measures about a yard, and although nearly two-thirds of this is tail, he is yet really a considerably bigger bird than the English pheasant; having a ten-inch wing, the shank nearly three inches, and the bill about half that.

The hen has the same dark cap and white throat, the former rather obscured by light edges to the feathers; but the neck and breast are black with pale edges, and the general body colour darker than in the cock, and rather mottled than barred, with longitudinal streaks of buff; the tail is also irregularly mottled and barred with brown, black, and buff; the lower part of the breast is plain chestnut edged with buff.

The hen is about two feet long or more, with a tail of over fourteen inches, and a wing of nine.

This is a well-known bird all through our hills, though somewhat local. With us it occurs from Chamba to Khatmandu, and it is not known outside these limits. It is a bird of moderate elevations, ranging between four and ten thousand feet according to seasons; it is particularly partial to wooded precipices, and very constant to localities which suit it. It is a sociable bird, flocks of from five to fifteen being commonly found, except in the breeding-season, and both sexes crow. The note is varied, but generally includes repetitions of the bird's name.

This pheasant is especially a root-eater, and it also feeds on berries, seeds, and insects, but not on leaves and grass. It breeds from April to June, laying up to fourteen eggs of a pale stone colour, usually speckled with brown at the end, and just over two inches long. The male Cheer has not been seen to show himself off to the female; but as one we had at the Calcutta Zoo used to assume a slanting posture, with his fine tail spread, when anxious to fight a visitor, I conclude that he was simply following the display habit of his species.

There now remain typical pheasants, belonging to the same genus as that which includes the well-known bird at home. In this group (*Phasianus*) both sexes are very similar in form, though they differ absolutely in colour; but the males are larger than the females, have short sharp spurs, and much longer tails. The tail in both sexes has the middle feathers much the longest, the others rapidly diminishing to the outer pair; and the long central feathers are transversely arched, so that they form a roof over the flat feathers below, the whole tail thus looking very narrow and pointed. The cocks have a red bare skin round the eye, and there is sometimes some of this in the hen. They show off in the sideway slanting posture. The pheasants of this group are active birds, strong on the wing and ready to rise: they will live anywhere where there is moderate cover, but avoid heavy forest. They are characteristic of temperate regions as a rule, and are the best game birds of the whole family.

Mrs. Hume's Pheasant.

Phasianus humiæ, Fauna Brit. Ind., Birds, Vol. IV, p. 80.

NATIVE NAME:—*Loe-nin-koi,* Manipur.

The general colour of the male in this species is a rich bay with a golden gloss; the head and neck are steel-blue, and the rump steel-blue with white edgings to each feather, giving a beautiful scaled appearance; there are two white bars across the wing, with a broad patch of steel-blue between them; the tail is grey, crossed by bars of mixed black and chestnut. The bill is greenish, eyes orange, and legs brown.

The hen is mottled with drab, sandy, and black, and has the outer pairs of tail-feathers chestnut with white tips, and imperfectly barred with black.

The male is about thirty-three inches long, about twenty inches being taken up by the tail;

the closed wing measures about eight and-a-half inches, and the shank nearly three. The hen has a very much shorter tail, this being only seven inches long; but her wing is only about half an inch less than the cock's.

Mr. Hume discovered this bird in Manipur in 1881. He only got two specimens, both males, and very few have since been procured. The species has, however, been found to also inhabit the Ruby Mines District in Upper Burma, as also the Shan States.

Burmese male birds commonly have the white edging of the rump-feather so much broader than in the typical birds, that the whole of that part of the back looks silver-white rather than scaled as in the ordinary form, but I do not consider them distinct, although Mr. Oates has named the Burmese bird—just distinguished as a variety by me—as a distinct species, *burmannicus*.

Elliot's Pheasant.

Phasianus ellioti, Brit. Mus. Cat., Birds, Vol. XXII, p. 335.

The male of this species, from the South-Eastern Chinese mountains, is readily distinguished from Hume's Pheasant by the white abdomen and white sides of the neck; the hen, in addition to the white abdomen, differs from the Hume's Pheasant hen by having a black throat. The eggs are pale buff. Unlike most pheasants, it is a wandering bird, and does not haunt one locality; it is well known in captivity in Europe.

Copper Pheasant.

Phasianus sommerringi, Brit. Mus. Cat., Birds, Vol. XXII, p. 336.

NATIVE NAME :—*Kee-ez*, Japanese.

The Copper Pheasant does not inhabit the whole of Japan, but only Hondo and Kiu-siu; the cock is chestnut in colour, with the edges of the back and breast feathers richly glossed with red-gold ; the tail which is a yard long, is in two shades of chestnut, barred with black. The hen is mottled with black and chestnut, with the tail, which is barely eight inches long, chestnut with black white tips. A variety of the cock, which has the golden edgings of the feathers replaced by black and white, has sometimes been distinguished as the Sparkling Pheasant, *P. scintillans.* The eggs are greenish-white ; the Japanese name expresses the peculiar call. This species in both varieties is well known in Europe ; but a third recently-described race or species, Ijima's Pheasant (*P. ijimæ*), from Kiu-siu, in which the whole rump of the cock is white, has not been imported, as far as I know.

Mikado Pheasant.

Calophasis mikado, Grant, Bull., Brit. Ornith. Club, Vol. XVI, p. 277.

Has only been recently made known ; the cock is one of the most distinct of all pheasants in appearance, and especially in this long-tailed group ; he is blue-black, with white markings on the wing, and white cross-bars on the tail. The hen is mottled brown, with small white dashes on the upper back and breast. The species inhabits Formosa.

Reeves' Pheasant.

Phasianus reevesi, Brit. Mus. Cat., Birds, Vol. XXII, p. 337.

This very beautiful species, familiar in captivity in Europe, and even sometimes kept at large there, is far bigger than any other long-tailed pheasant, the hen even being as large as the cocks of the ordinary pheasants. The cock has an excessively long tail—five or six feet ; this is chiefly silver-grey, boldly barred with black ; the head and neck are black and white, with very little red skin round the eye ; the upper parts yellow, with black edges to the feathers. The hen is very minutely and beautifully variegated with black, buff and grey like a Nightjar ; her head is buff, with dark-brown crown and eye-stripes, and there are white dashes on the upper back and breast ; the middle tail-feathers, which are not longer proportionately than in common pheasants, are mottled grey, the outside ones mostly chestnut, tipped with white. This bird is wild and flies for long distances ; the cock's note is like the warble of a small bird. It inhabits the mountains of North and West China.

Stone's Pheasant.

Phasianus elegans, Fauna Brit. Ind., Vol. IV, p. 81.

The male of this species has a great general resemblance to the common English pheasant, having the same green and purple head and neck, and chestnut upper back and flanks, the latter spangled with purple black; the tail also is similar, light brown with black bars. But the small wing-coverts, which are sandy in the English pheasant, are French-grey in the present bird, which also has the rump or lower back gray and green instead of maroon. Moreover, the glossy green-black of the lower breast extends in this species right up to the green neck, whereas in the home pheasant the upper breast is bay with purple edgings to the feathers.

The legs are lead-coloured, and the bare skin of the face scarlet. The hen is mottled with black and pale drab, much like the hen of the well-known pheasant at home. The absence of chestnut on the outer tail-feathers will distinguish her from the hen of Hume's Pheasant.

The cock is about twenty-seven inches long, with a nine-inch wing and sixteen-inch tail; the shank is about two and-a-half inches, and the bill one and-a-quarter. The hen is decidedly smaller, with a much shorter tail in proportion, this measuring only nine inches—an inch longer than her closed wing.

This pheasant was first known from the province of Szechuen in Southern China, but was almost simultaneously found by Dr. J. Anderson the first Superintendent of the Indian Museum at Momien in the Yunnan province, where it was common on grassy hills at an elevation of five thousand feet. Recently it has turned up in Burma, at about the same elevation, in the Northern Shan States, where one was shot by Lieutenant H. R. Wallis.

There is considerable difference of opinion as to exactly how many species or races of the pheasants of this type are to be recognised; but the following are easily distinguishable and well known :—

Common Pheasant.

Phasianus colchicus, Brit. Mus. Cat., Birds, Vol. XXII, p. 322.

This species ranges from Greece to through Asia Minor and Transcaucasia, and is still common in the vicinity of the ancient Phasis (the modern River Rion, in Mingrelia), whence, classical tradition says, it was imported into Europe. The pure bird, in addition to the absence of white neck-ring and to having sandy wings, is distinguished by having the rump dark maroon red, with no green or grey tinge; the eggs are olive in colour.

Ring-Necked Pheasant.

Phasianus torquatus, Brit. Mus. Cat., Birds, Vol. XXII, p. 331.

This is the characteristic Pheasant of China, ranging from the Lower Amoor to Canton; it has been known in Britain for more than a century. The pure Chinese bird has white eyebrows and collar, grey wings and rump, and the flanks distinctly paler than the breast, being buff; the Formosan race (*P. formosanus*) has their primrose-colour. The hen is drab, mottled with black, like that of the Common Pheasant.

Green Japanese Pheasant.

Phasianus versicolor, Brit. Mus. Cat., Birds, Vol. XXII, p. 324.

This is far the most distinct in colour of all the races; it is confined to Japan, and even there does not occur in Yezo. The breast and flanks are all dark glossy green, the wings and rump grey; there is no neck-ring. The hen is more darkly mottled with black than in other hen pheasants of this type, especially on the breast. This is well known in Europe, and often crossed with the two previous races. Stone's pheasant much resembles the hybrid thus produced.

Mongolian Pheasant.

Phasianus mongolicus, Brit. Mus. Cat., Birds, Vol. XXII, p. 328.

This species, ranging from the Syr-Darya east to lake Zaisan and south to the Issik-kul valley, is very distinct from the three last in two structural points—the absence of the ear-tufts and the fact that the naked red face-skin only dilates below the eye and not above also. In colour it is dark coppery red, with the darker markings on breast and flanks indistinct; there is a broad white collar, interrupted in front by the copper-red of the breast, which runs up the neck, this not being green or purple all round as in other pheasants of this type; the white wings and straw-coloured eyes are also striking points. The light eyes also characterise the hen which is also paler than the hens of the common and Ring-necked species. The Dzungarian race (*P. semitorquatus*) is similar, but has a green instead of purple gloss on the plumage, and the collar more widely broken. The Mongolian is a large race, and greatly favoured at present in Britain for crossing purposes.

Royal or Murghab Pheasant.

Phasianus principalis, Brit. Mus. Cat., Birds, Vol. XXII, p. 325.

This species is of particular interest to Indian sportsmen, as it is found in North-West Afghanistan, ranging into the adjacent parts of Persia. It is, like the Common Pheasant, rather uniform in tint and devoid of a white collar, but is light in hue, being chestnut rather than bay, and has the wing-coverts white. The hen is lighter than that of the Common Pheasant. In the bed of the Bala Murghab river, where it was discovered, it leads a semi-aquatic life, running and swimming in watery thickets like a Rail. It has of late been introduced into Britain. I use the name "Royal" as it was named after the late King Edward VII when Prince of Wales.

Besides these, there are two very distinct races which have not been introduced to Europe so far as I know :—

Oxus Pheasant.

Phasianus chrysomelas, Brit. Mus. Cat., Birds, Vol. XXII, p. 327.

This race, from the Amu-Darya valley, has the spangling of the flanks very large and bold, and dark green : the green edgings of the breast feathers coalesce and fuse with the green of the neck ; there is no white neck-ring, but the wings are white ; the rump is reddish. The hen is pale, like that of the Mongolian.

Vlangal's Pheasant.

Phasianus ulangali, Brit. Mus. Cat., Birds, Vol. XXII, p. 330.

Vlangal's Pheasant inhabits the Tsaidam marshes, but so remarkably pale in colour, suggesting a desert form ; the shoulders are sandy, without the usual markings, and the ground-colour of the flanks buff ; the wings and rump grey as in the Ring-neck, but there is no neck-ring, the hen is very pale, the dark mottlings of the plumage being fawn, instead of black as in other hens of this type.

Then there are several less distinct forms closely related to the above.

Shaw's Pheasant.

Phasianus shawi, Brit. Mus. Cat., Birds, Vol. XXII, p. 326.

This is the Yarkand race, and comes very near to the Murghab Pheasant, but has, among other small differences, a tinge of grey on the wings and green on the rump.

Persian Pheasant.

Phasianus persicus, Brit. Mus. Cat., Birds, Vol. XXII, p. 324.

The Persian race comes nearest the Common Pheasant, but is rather lighter and has the wing-coverts nearly white, thus approaching the Murghab race ; the hen, however, is as dark as that of the Common Pheasant. The Pheasants of the Zerafshan and Tarim valleys (*P. zerafshanicus* and *P. tarimensis*) are sub-races of this form.

Strauch's Pheasant.

Phasianus strauchi, Brit. Mus. Cat., Birds, Vol, XXII, p. 330.

Strauch's Pheasant, from the mountains of Kan-su and Sze-chuen, is somewhat like the Common Pheasant, but has grey wing-coverts and the rump grey and green, thus approaching the Ring-neck ; the sub-race *P. berezowskyi* differs but little.

Hagenbeck's Pheasant.

Phasianus hagenbecki, Rothschild, Bull. Brit. Ornith. Club, Vote XII, p. 20.

Is a paler and more distinctly marked race of the Ring-neck, from Mongolia ; it ranges the furthest north of these pheasants, as the typical Ring-neck goes furthest south; the Satschuen Pheasant (*P. satschuensis*) is also a pale Ring-neck.

Collarless Pheasant.

Phasianus decollatus, Brit. Mus. Cat., Birds, Vol. XXII, p. 331.

This bird, from East Yunnan and West China, is much like the Chinese Ring-neck, but has the white collar absent or only just indicated, and the breast-feather with broader dark margins.

Many more races have been described, M. Buturlin naming twice as many as are described here ; but in a book intended for sportsmen, as this is, it is unnecessary to go into details about them ; it will have been seen already that, as it is, except for half-a-dozen or so, these local forms are hard to make out, and even the best characterised races breed so freely together that their distinction as species is very doubtful,

CHAPTER V.

Koklass and Kaleeges.

The Koklass, although they come under the heading of pheasants with medium tails, bear a stronger general resemblance to some of the long-tailed species I have been dealing with. Both sexes have the head entirely feathered, and the body-feathers pointed in shape. The tail is pointed, both with regard to its individual feathers and its general shape, the centre feathers being the longest and the outside the shortest. The wings are longer and more pointed than in any other pheasants, the primary or pinion-quills showing noticeably beyond the secondaries when the wing is closed, unlike what is usually the case in this family.

The cocks are altogether different in colour from the hens, and stand higher on the leg, which in them is spurred. They have, however, only one piece of special feather-ornamentation, though this is a sufficiently remarkable one; for it consists in the male having *three* crests, one long one growing from the crown, and two still longer, which flank it on each side. I have never seen any description of the display of the males, but it ought to be interesting. The hens have a short ordinary crest.

The Common Koklass or Pukras.

Pucrasia macrolopha, Fauna Brit. Ind., Birds, Vol. IV, p. 85.

NATIVE NAMES :—*Plas*, Kashmir ; *Kukrola*, Chamba ; *Koak*, Kulu, Mandi ; *Koklass*, *Kokla*, Simla to Almora ; *Pokras*, Kumaun, Garhwal and W. Nepal.

The cock of this species has a dark green head, with the central crest fawn-colour, and a white spot at each side at the commencement of the neck. The front of the neck is chestnut, and this colour extends right down the breast and belly, becoming paler behind. The rest of the body plumage is streaked with black and grey, the former colour occupying the centre of the feathers, and the latter the edges. The centre tail-feathers are reddish brown, and the others black with narrow white tips, and running into chestnut towards the root.

The Koklass, however, is a very variable species, especially with regard to the breadth of the chestnut colouring on the under-parts and the proportions of the black and grey in the body feathers. In the typical bird, as found in the N.-W. Himalayas, the black centre stripe is about as wide as the grey edging, but in Western Nepal specimens the black is much increased, and the chestnut shows a tendency to extend to the back and sides of the neck. But the two forms run into each other. Again, the race from Western Kashmir combines this extension of the chestnut neck colour with the narrow black stripes of the type. All these variations have been named as species, the North-West Himalayan bird being the true *Pucra-*

sia macrolopha, while the dark Nepal form is *P. nepalensis*, and the Kashmir bird *P. biddulphi*.

The length of the cock is about two feet, with the wing just over nine inches and the tail about ten; the shank measures about two and-a-half inches and the bill about one and-a-half.

The hen is mottled with black and brown, with buff streaks above; her eyebrows are buff, and her throat pure white; below she is buff with black streaks, and the middle of the belly white; the side tail-feathers are black, tipped with white and edged with chestnut outside. The hens are much the same everywhere, except that in the Nepal variety there is often much more chestnut in the tail.

The short, flat, pointed tail, feathered face, and long wings will easily distinguish the hen Koklass from other hen pheasants.

She is about three inches shorter than the male, with an eight-inch tail, and wing only a little longer; the shank is two and-a-quarter inches.

The Koklass is confined to the Himalayas, from Jumla in Western Nepal to Kashmir; its range is from about four thousand feet to the forest limits. It is pre-eminently a forest bird, and lies close till flushed, when it flies with great rapidity and is hard to shoot. Although living on a mixed diet like most pheasants, it has an especial preference for leaves and buds; it is supposed to be our best pheasant for the table.

It has apparently named itself, like so many Indian birds, the crow of the male being compared to the words "*kok-kok pokrass.*" He usually crows in the morning and evening, but will also answer a gunshot or a peal of thunder—a not uncommon habit with pheasants.

The breeding season is from April to June, and the birds are then found in pairs; in autumn and winter they collect into coveys.

The eggs are about nine in number, pale buff, often marked with reddish spots of varying size, and two inches long. No nest of any sort is made, the eggs being deposited in a "scrape" on the ground.

The Chestnut Koklass.

Pucrasia castanea, Blandford, Faun. Brit. Ind., Vol. IV, p. 86.

I mention this species because it is believed to occur in our Empire; but very little is known about it, only two specimens, now in the British Museum, having ever been obtained. These are said to have been obtained from Kafiristan, and the bird is also credited with inhabiting Yassin, Chitral, and Swat.

It differs from the common Koklass in the much greater extension of the chestnut colour, which runs all round the neck, extends some way down the back and covers the flanks as well as the breast; the middle of the belly being black.

The hen appears to be still unknown, so that there is a good deal to be made out about the species yet. Of course, there is always the possibility of its turning out to be a mere rufous variety of the common Koklass, just as the Nepal bird is a dark variety. The common grey partridge of Europe (*Perdix cinerea*), which has certainly not more chestnut in its plumage than the ordinary Koklass possesses, sometimes produces a variety —formerly named as a species, *Perdix montana*— which may be of a rich chestnut colour almost all over.

Meyer's Koklass.

Pucrasia meyeri, Brit. Mus. Cat., Birds, Vol. XXII, p. 315.

The cock of this species is very like the Common Indian Koklass, but has a yellow collar at the back of the neck; the hen is distinguished by having the outer tail-feathers nearly all chestnut. It extends from the Mekong river to Central Tibet.

Yellow-necked Koklass.

Pucrasia xanthospila, Brit. Mus. Cat., Birds, Vol. XXII, p. 315; *Song-ky*, Chinese.

This has a buff or chestnut collar, but can be distinguished from both Meyer's Koklass and the common species by having the outer tail-feathers grey, barred with black; this point will also distinguish the hen. It ranges from North-west China to Eastern Tibet, in the mountains.

Darwin's Koklass.

Pucrasia darwini, Brit. Mus. Cat., Birds, Vol. XXII, p. 316; *Song-ky*, Chinese.

In this species, the sides of the cock are buff in the ground-colour, with black longitudinal bands; he has no buff colour. The hen is most like that of the last species, but has the bars on the tail-feathers only scantily represented by spots. It inhabits the Eastern Chinese mountains.

Styan's Koklass.

Pucrasia styani, Grant, Bull. Brit. Ornith. Club, XXIII, p. 32.

This species, from Ichang in Central China, has the under-parts streaked black and grey throughout, with no central belt of chestnut like all the other species; above it most resembles the last. The hen is not known.

The Kaleeges form a large genus of pheasants which are very easily recognisable. In all, both sexes have a crest, and the sides of the face covered with bare red skin, which, in the cocks at all events, is extensible upwards and downwards. The tails in all the species are folded like that of a common fowl, and in most of them are not much longer than an ordinary hen's tail; but in the males the top feathers have a decided curve, and in some of the species the tail is quite long in that sex. The cocks are well spurred, and are hard fighters; they have a curious habit of buzzing with their wings as a challenge.

As sporting birds, the Kaleeges are not to be commended. They won't rise if they can possibly help it, and as they live in jungle, can make their arrangements for skulking in safety, and do so. They do not range so high as the other pheasants, and sometimes even inhabit the plains.

To the naturalist some of the species are of the highest interest, as they exhibit so many gradations that it is doubtful how many kinds there really are. This, however, is not encouraging to the beginner who wishes to precisely identify whatever birds he may get. It is very probable that a good deal of interbreeding goes on, with the natural result of the production of a set of mongrels, since the crosses bred from these nearly allied birds are probably fertile.

About the first three species there is, however, no doubt; the males of these all have tails much like an ordinary domestic hen's, as described above, and their plumage is always black, or rather steel-blue above, and greyish white below, the white feathers of the under-surface being conspicuously pointed. Their legs are never red or pink.

The hens of these species are all very much alike, hardly to be distinguished at all in fact. Their tails are almost completely fowl-like and their crests narrow and projecting; their plumage is of a nut-brown, with light shafts and tips to the feathers; the tail feathers, except the centre or uppermost pair, are black. The plumage has a much more uniform appearance than that of other hen pheasants, the light markings being so small that the birds appear plain brown by comparison with these.

The White-crested Kaleege.

Gennæus albicristatus, Faun. Brit. Ind., Birds, Vol. IV, p. 89.

NATIVE NAMES:—*Kalij*, *Kukera*, *Mirghi Kalij*, *Kalesur* (male), *Kalesi* (female), Hind. in the N.-W. Himalayas; *Kolsa*, in the N. Punjab and Chamba.

The male of this species has a long, narrow drooping crest of white hairy-looking feathers; his upper plumage is black, glossed with blue, and his tail black; the rump is barred with white, the feathers being white-tipped, and most of the under-surface is dirty white, the throat and belly being brown. The hen is brown, as above described.

The bill of this bird is greenish white, and the legs dirty white also. The cock measures from two to two and-a-half feet in length, of which the tail is about a foot. The wing is over nine inches, the shank three, and the bill about one and-a-half. The hen ranges from about two feet down to twenty inches, her tail and wing being each about eight inches long.

This species inhabits a zone, from two to ten thousand feet in elevation, according to the season, from Kumaun to Hazara in the Himalayas; it is said not to be found west of the Indus, and of Nepal it only penetrates the westernmost portion, if it is found in that country at all. Of all the hill pheasants this most affects the neighbourhood of man; but it is nevertheless not easy to domesticate. It breeds from April to June, the hen laying about nine cream-coloured eggs in a rude grass nest on the ground. The eggs are about two inches long.

The Nepal Kaleege.

Gennæus leucomelanus, Blanford, Faun. Brit. Ind., Birds, Vol. IV, p. 90.

NATIVE NAMES:—*Kalij*, Hindi; *Rechabo*, Bhutia.

This species is blue-black above and white below, with a white-barred rump, like the last; but it has a black crest. The hens are practically indistinguishable, and the dimensions differ very little, though the present species is slightly the smaller. The legs are horny grey, darker than in the white-crested Kaleege; the face of course red, as usual in this group.

This is the only Kaleege found in most parts of Nepal; its nesting habits and eggs appear not to be recorded.

The Black-backed Kaleege.

Gennæus melanonotus, Faun. Brit. Ind., Birds, Vol. IV, p. 91.

NATIVE NAME :—*Kar-rhyak*, Lepcha.

This species resembles the last in size and in having a black crest, but differs in having the upper surface entirely rich blue-black, with no white edgings on the rump; the hen is like that of the preceding species.

The present bird inhabits the Sikkim Himalayas, extending on the one side into Eastern Nepal and on the other into Bhutan, but its exact range is not yet known. It is, like the others, a bird of moderate elevations. It breeds from March to July, according to the elevation it inhabits, and apparently differs from the white-crested Kaleege in making no nest at all and often laying fewer eggs.

As will have been seen, the Nepal Kaleege is intermediate in colour—as it is in geographical range—between this species and the white-crested, having the black crest of the present bird and the white-barred rump of the white-crested species. It has therefore been suspected of being a hybrid between these two by Blyth and Jerdon, but the researches of Dr. Scully have removed the bar sinister from its escutcheon.

The males of all the kaleeges now to be dealt with differ markedly from those previously described, in having the breast-feathers of the ordinary rounded shape, not narrow and pointed. Moreover, the breast is always mostly black, generally completely so. It is about the species of this section that so much uncertainty exists.

The Black-breasted or Purple Kaleege.

Gennæus horsfieldi, Faun. Brit. Ind., Birds, Vol. IV, p. 92.

NATIVE NAMES :—*Mathura*, Chittagong and Sylhet ; *Dúrúg*, *Dirrik*, Garo Hills ; *Dorik*, at Dibrugarh ; the last name seems commonly used by Europeans.

This is a bird of similar type to the light-breasted kaleeges hitherto dealt with, with a narrow projecting crest, and rather short hen-like tail. The cock is altogether of a glossy purple-black, except for the white barring on the rump which he has in common with two of his allies above mentioned.

The hen is just like the hens of the previous kaleeges—brown, with each feather tipped with a lighter shade, and with the tail-feathers black, except the top or central pair.

The bill is horn-colour, face red, and legs drab or grey.

The dimensions are also as in the previous species, the cock being about two feet long and the hen about twenty inches. This bird's range extends from the lower hills of East Bhootan and the Daphla country, north of the Assam valley, throughout the ranges to the southward to Chittagong, North Arrakan, South Manipur and Bhamo. Its eggs, which resemble those of the preceding kaleeges, have been found in Sylhet towards the end of March. It has been tried as a game-bird in English preserves, but though it throve well, was killed off again as a nuisance, being very pugnacious to the true pheasants, hard to put up, and flying dangerously low for shooting when it could be made to rise.

The Lineated Kaleege or Burmese Silver Pheasant.

Gennæus lineatus, Faun. Brit. Ind., Birds, Vol. IV, p. 92.

NATIVE NAMES :—*Yit*, *Kayit*, Burmese; *Rak*, Arrakanese; *Synklouk*, Talain; *Phugyk*, Karen.

This is a slightly larger bird than the last, but of the same type as regards the narrow stiffish crest and rather short tail; its colouration is, however, of a quite different character.

The male is blue-black only on the crest and on the under-parts; the flanks are also black, with white streaks in the centres of the feathers, which streaking may extend over all of the breast also. But the upper plumage, wings, and tail, are of a grizzly grey or pepper-and-salt colour, produced by fine zig-zag black and white pencillings, which get stronger and coarser on the quills of the wing and tail. The topmost or centre tail-feathers, however, are pure white on their inner webs and tips, contrasting well with the rest of the plumage.

The hen is brown, with the head, neck, upper back, and breast distinctly streaked with white, the white marks being V-shaped on the back of the neck and shoulders. Her centre tail-feathers have the inner webs and the tips buff, corresponding to the white of the same pair in the cock; and the outer pairs are black, marked with brown, and pencilled with wavy white lines. She is thus easily distinguishable from the hens of the previous species.

The face is red, as usual, in this species, and the bill greenish horn-colour; the eyes, however, vary from red-brown to white, and the legs from drab to flesh-colour.

This is the kaleege of Burma, and it extends to south-western Siam. It frequents hilly grounds, and keeps to cover, being an inveterate runner and skulker. It breeds in March and April, the nest being merely a hollow lined with a few dead leaves, and containing seven eggs of a pale buff colour.

In order to understand the kaleeges of this group, it will be necessary to describe a species which is not Indian, but which with the extension of our Empire or of its own ranges may come to be a British subject, and is at all events better known generally than any other kaleege.

This is the Silver Pheasant (*Gennæus nycthemerus*) of China (Brit. Mns. Cat., Birds, Vol. XXII, p. 307) now rare in a wild state in that country, but very widely known as an aviary bird, as it thrives better than any other pheasant in captivity. In this bird, which is larger than any of our species, the male has a long full drooping crest, and a very long tail reaching two feet, and gracefully arched and tapered ; but the feathers composing the tail are flat and lie vertically and back to back as in other kaleeges. The crest, under-parts, and flanks in the cock are blue-black, and the upper plumage, wings and tail pure white, with fine hair-like black pencilling, which becomes strong and bold on the wings and side tail-feathers. The centre tail-feathers are plain, and at a little distance the whole upper plumage looks white.

The hen has a very short black crest and a moderately long, closely-folded tail. She is of a plain uniform brown, with the side tail-feathers boldly pencilled with black and white.

Both sexes have bright red legs, pale green bills, and red faces, the male's face having a beautiful velvety appearance.

Crawfurd's or Anderson's Silver Pheasant.

Gennæus andersoni, Faun. Brit. Ind., Birds, Vol. IV, p. 94.

This species, which is rather doubtful and has been described under several names, is intermediate between the two last. The tail of the male, although not so long as that of the Silver Pheasant of China, is nevertheless considerably longer than the wing, and curved ; the crest is full and drooping. This crest, with the under-parts and flanks, is black with a blue gloss, as usual ; the upper parts appear grey at a little distance, but close at hand are seen to be boldly and clearly marked with concentric lines of black and white, equal in breadth and resembling a curved V or a Gothic arch in shape. The accuracy of the pattern is something remarkable, and has a very beautiful effect. On the quills of the wing and tail the marking becomes a rather irregular pencilling, and on the inner webs and tips of the middle tail-feathers the black pencilling dies away altogether.

The hen is plain brown almost throughout, including the side tail-feathers, but is marked on the breast with V-shaped white streaks.

The cock is two and-a-half to three feet long, of which more than half is tail. The wing measures about ten inches.

This is one of the doubtful species to which I alluded above, as are also those which follow. Only a few specimens have been obtained, and these appear to differ considerably. The type of the species, however, obtained by the late Dr. Anderson in the Kachin Hills, closely agrees with birds from the Ruby Mines in Burma and with others obtained by French naturalists from Annam. I was able to observe the last in Paris some years ago, and there saw the hen. Dr. Anderson's bird, which was in my time still in the Indian Museum, had flesh-coloured legs, but the others I have seen had red ones like the Chinese Silver Pheasant. Several skins collected by Captain W. G. Nisbett in the Kachin Hills, north of Bhamo and east of Myitkyina, show the most remarkable gradations between this species and the Purple or Black-breasted Kaleege (*Gennæus horsfieldi*), and the two species evidently interbreed there, the Purple Kaleege strain predominating on the lower ground and the Silver Pheasant on the higher. One such hybrid, with the white pencilling on the upper surface less strong than in the true *andersoni* and showing white rump-bars, has been called *Gennæus davisoni*. Mr. Oates considers this form the true *andersoni*, and calls the Ruby Mines birds *Gennæus rufipes*. All I can say is, however, that what I have above described as *G. andersoni* corresponds with the typical specimen in Calcutta and with the figures which have been published to accompany accounts of that species, so that there should be no doubt about it.

Blanford, in the *Fauna of British India*, suggests that *G. andersoni* may after all only be a cross between the Lineated Kaleege and the Chinese Silver Pheasant; and certainly there is a stuffed specimen of this cross in the Paris Museum which no body could call anything else but an Anderson's Silver Pheasant if they did not know its origin. On the other hand, the uniformity of the type in several specimens might be used as an argument for its distinctness. Many hybrids, however, are known to be very uniform in type, especially those between the Golden and Amherst Pheasants, and the goldfinch and bullfinch. Moreover, intermediate forms appear to occur between Anderson's and the Lineated Pheasant, and also between the former and the true Chinese Silver Pheasant, so that on our eastern frontiers there seems to be a great deal of confusion among these birds which has not yet been cleared up. Experimental breeding in confinement ought to settle the matter, and with birds so easily kept and studied as are the kaleeges the problem might be solved in a few years.

I have dwelt on this point at such length because the same remarks apply to the other doubtful forms I shall now describe, though none of these are so interesting as the Anderson's Silver Pheasant, which is really a very beautiful bird in its own way and quite unlike anything else, so that if it really is a hybrid, it is a very remarkable product.

Cuvier's Kaleege.

Gennæus cuvieri, Faun. Brit. Ind., Birds, Vol. IV, p. 93.

In this bird, which exactly resembles the Purple Kaleege in shape, the plumage is also much like that of that bird, being mostly purple-black with white bars on the rump; but the upper parts, wings, and tail are all regularly but finely pencilled with white lines. The marking, in fact, is that of the Chinese Silver Pheasant reversed. All the tail-feathers are pencilled in this way, from the centre pair to the outside, whereas in most of these pencilled pheasants the marking differs on the different feathers of the tail.

The hen is brown with lighter edges to the feathers, like that of the Purple Kaleege, but her outer tail-feathers, instead of being plain black as in the hen of that species, are pencilled with fine white lines like the plumage of her own mate.

This species, which resembles the Purple Kaleege in size, seems to be found in the most typical form in the Chin Hills; at any rate, some specimens I have examined from there agree remarkably in their plumage. The figure given by Temminck, who first described *Gennæus cuvieri*, also agrees closely with the Chin Hills birds; but Temminck could give no locality for his specimen.

At the same time, these Chin Hills kaleeges with fine white pencilling on black may be merely hybrids between the Purple and the Lineated Kaleege as Blanford thought. They certainly are just what one might expect from such a cross.

Oates's Kaleege.

Gennæus oatesi, Faun. Brit. Ind., Birds, Vol. IV, p. 94.

This is still more like the Purple Kaleege, not only resembling it in shape and size, but being almost completely blue-black with white rump-bars. But there is on the upper plumage a scanty and broken pencilling, or rather peppering, of white, giving it a frosted appearance; and the inner webs of the middle tail-feathers are nearly white, as in the Lineated Kaleege.

The hen is like that of the Purple Kaleege, but has the black outer tail-feathers mottled with black and chestnut, and the inner webs of the centre tail-feathers pale buff or cream-colour.

This seems to be the kaleege of the Arrakan Hills, two of Blyth's old specimens in the Asiatic Society's collection deposited in the Indian Museum agreeing with the above description. The description which Blanford gives of *G. cuvieri* in the place above cited, also agrees better in some respects with this bird than with Temminck's. But he considers this form also a hybrid, as did Blyth, who identified it with Temminck's *G. cuvieri*. And two other specimens of Blyth's from Arrakan are most obviously hybrids between the Purple and Lineated Kaleeges.

Many other pencilled kaleeges have been described, but I have contented myself with noting the forms I have been able to make out personally; as, except the Purple, Silver, and Lineated birds, all the species with which we are here concerned are very doubtful. Sportsmen who are interested in the subject should preserve, however roughly, the skin of any pencilled kaleege they may shoot in out-of-the-way places, or at least take photographs of such, the black and white markings lending themselves admirably to photographic reproduction. The dimensions and locality should of course be noted. By the collection of such evidence we may at length find out how many species there really are, but I fancy experimental breeding would determine the point a good deal sooner.

Whitehead's Silver Pheasant.

Gennæus whiteheadi, Grant, Proc., Zool. Soc., 1900, p. 503.

This bears a general resemblance to the Chinese Silver Pheasant above described, but has the upper surface with bold but scanty black pencilling, only one pair of thick curved lines on each feather, joining near the tip; the black markings on the wings and outer tail-feathers are also stronger. The hen is much more different from that of the Silver Pheasant, having the neck and under-parts white with black edges to the feathers, and the tail all brown. The bird is confined to Hainan.

Swinhoe's Kaleege.

Gennæus swinhoii, Brit. Mus. Cat., Birds, Vol. XXII, p. 309.

Confined to Formosa, this species is the most distinct of all. The cock is rich purple-black, with the short crest, centre tail-feathers, and upper back, pure white and the shoulders deep glossy red. The hen is variegated with brown and buff, with the outer tail-feathers bay. The face and legs are red. It is well known in captivity in Europe.

The Fire-backed Pheasant.

Lophura rufa, Faun. Brit. Ind., Birds, Vol. IV, p. 87.

After such a terribly mixed up lot as the pencilled kaleeges, it is a relief to come across a bird which is very distinct from everything else, as is the present one. In its general appearance the Fireback resembles the shorter-tailed kaleeges, but the male has a different style of crest, this being erect and brushlike, and composed of feathers which are bare-shafted at the base. There does not, indeed, seem much reason for separating the few species of Firebacks from the kaleege genus. In the male of our only species, the general colour of the plumage is metallic-purple; the lower back is fiery copper-red, and the two centre pairs of tail-feathers and part of the next pair are white. There are also some white streaks on the sides of the body.

The hen is chestnut-coloured with white edges to the feathers of the neck in front; below this the feathers are black, still with white edges, and the pattern extends along the flanks; the centre of the belly is plain white.

The bare skin of the face is bright blue and the eyes red; the bill all white in the male, but brown below in the female. The legs and feet are bright red.

The cock is a large bird, measuring twenty-eight inches in length, of which less than a foot goes to the tail; the wing is almost a foot long, and the shank nearly five inches. The hen is less than two feet long, with a ten-inch wing and tail of only eight inches.

This pheasant only just comes within our area, inhabiting Sumatra and the Malay Peninsula, whence it extends into the most southern part of Tenasserim. It inhabits evergreen forests, and is found in small parties of about half-a-dozen, though the males are sometimes solitary. They buzz with their wings like the kaleeges. Like them also, they are vicious birds; a very fine specimen shown me by a native gentleman in Calcutta, which had been kept for more than twelve years, was confined in a cage for attacking one of the servants—whose wrist it had ripped open with its spur—when allowed to run at large. Another of the species, in Rutledge's possession and also allowed liberty, was, when I last saw it, walking round and round an old native in a manner which boded an attack. It was interesting to see that the bird's fighting attitude was exactly like what would be the show position before a hen. The blue face-skin was expanded, and the slanting pose assumed, so as to keep the copper back always in full view of the spectator on whom the bird was intent.

Little seems to be known of the Fire-back altogether; our information about its breeding has been furnished by a captive hen, which laid, in July, a buff egg a little over two inches long.

Bornean Fire-back.

Lophura ignita, Brit. Mus. Cat., Birds, Vol. XXII, p. 288; *Sempidan*, in Sarawak.

This has a general resemblance to the last, but differs conspicuously by having the upper tail-feathers buff and the under-parts below the breast of an old-gold colour. The legs are white. The hen is darker on the back than the hen *rufa*, and has a black tail. The species is confined to Borneo.

An intermediate form between *rufa* and *ignita*, known only from two captive specimens, has only some chestnut markings on the sides of the under-parts, and the upper tail-feathers white; it is not known whether this is a distinct species, a hybrid, or a "sport" of *L. ignita*.

Diard's Fire-back.

Lophura diardi, Brit. Mus. Cat., Birds, Vol. XXII, p. 290.

This fire-back is a much smaller bird than the rest, being smaller than the common English Pheasant, and slenderly built; it also has the face-skin red instead of blue, and the bare shafts of the crest are longer. Its general colour is grey, with a gold patch on the lower back, the rump glossy crimson, with blue edges to the feathers, and the head and tail black; the legs are red. The hen is reddish brown with buff and black bars on the wings and the belly black with white edgings. This lovely bird inhabits the Shan States, and ranges to Cochin China; it is much kept in captivity in Europe.

Wattled Pheasant.

Lobiophasis bulweri, Brit. Mus. Cat., Birds, Vol. XXII, p. 292; *Bagier*, Sarawak.

This splendid member of the Kaleege group occupies a genus to itself; it is about the size of the common Kaleeges, with a long curved tail, composed of no less than 32 pointed feathers, in the male, which is of a deep metallic-blue with the tail pure white and neck deep red; the head is nearly covered with blue bare skin produced into three pairs of wattles, and the legs are red. The hen has a much shorter tail, and is brown with fine black mottling. Young cocks have brighter red necks and shorter cinnamon tails. The species is only found in the mountains of Sarawak.

A curious genus of Kaleeges (*Acomus*) in which there is no crest, and the tail in both sexes is folded and short, just like that of a common hen, may be called crestless Kaleeges. The hens are black, and look much like black fowls without combs. They all have red bare faces, and are about the size of ordinary Kaleeges. Three species are known.

Malayan Crestless Kaleege.

Acomus erythrophthalmus, Brit. Mus. Cat., Birds, Vol. XXII, p. 283.

The cock is blue-black with fine white pencilling, a gold and red patch on the lower back, and a chestnut tail. This bird inhabits the Malay Peninsula, South of Indian limits, and Sumatra.

Bornean Crestless Kaleege.

Acomus pyronotus, Brit. Mus. Cat., Birds, Vol. XXII, p. 284; *Singgier*, Borneo.

This differs from the last by the grey neck, pencilled with black, and in the white shaft-streaks on the neck and breast; the hens of the two are alike. It inhabits Sarawak.

Black Crestless Kaleege.

Acomus inornatus, Brit. Mus. Cat., Birds, Vol. XXII, p. 285; *Ajam mera muta*, Sumatra.

As its name implies, this species is black all over, at least in the cock; the hen is unknown. It is found in Sumatra, on Mount Singallan and the Padang highlands.

The Eared-Pheasants (*Crossoptilon*) of Central Asia and China are large, fine, heavily-built birds, of the size of Monauls, with large tails, shaped much like that of a common hen, but with the feathers peculiarly filmy and fringe-like; the whole plumage is more or less of this texture, and there is no sex-difference in colour, though the males alone have spurs. The throat in all is white and the cap black, and there are white tufts standing up like ears on each side of the head, whence the name of the group. All have bare red faces and red feet. There are only five species.

The White Eared-Pheasant.

Crossoptilon tibetanum, Brit. Mus. Cat., Vol. XXII, p. 293.

This species has the plumage for the most part white, but the tail is glossy blue-black. It inhabits high elevations in East Tibet and West China.

The White-tailed Eared-Pheasant.

Crossoptilon leucurum, Brit. Mus. Cat., Vol. XXII, p. 294.

This East-Tibetan species only differs from the last in the male in having the tail only blue-black at the tip, the base being white; in the female the dark parts of the tail-feathers are slate-colour. It may ultimately be proved to be only a local race or variety of the last.

The Blue Eared-Pheasant.

Crossoptilon auritum, Brit. Mus. Cat., Vol. XXII, p. 295.

Ranges from Kokonor to East Szechuen, and is mainly blue-grey, with the tail white, tipped with black. It lives in mountain woods and lays olive-grey eggs.

Harman's Eared-Pheasant.

Crossoptilon harmani, Brit. Mus. Cat., Vol. XXII, p. 296.

Differs from the last in having more white about the head and neck and hardly any on the tail. The only known specimen was got 150 miles east of Lhassa.

Brown Eared-Pheasant.

Crossoptilon mantchuricum, Brit. Mus. Cat., Vol. XXII, p. 294.

Inhabits the mountains of Manchuria and Pe-che-lee, and is mainly sooty brown in colour, with the tail white, tipped with blue-black. It has been fairly freely imported into Europe and breeds well in captivity, laying pale stone-coloured eggs

CHAPTER VI.

Partridges.

With the birds discussed in the last chapter the series of pheasants comes to an end, and we enter on the consideration of the various partridges. These are, as was said in the Introduction, short-tailed birds, usually much smaller than pheasants. They fall into several very natural generic groups, some containing only one Indian species each. There is some difficulty for the beginner in making them out, for the males are generally plain and much like the females, and do not present those striking characteristics which make the various cock pheasants referable to their proper genera at once. But with a little trouble partridges are not more difficult correctly to identify than are hen pheasants.

Taking as partridges all the short-tailed game birds with a wing over five inches long—under that size they rank as quails—we find that they may again be subdivided, as were the pheasants, by the length of tail. All partridges have rather short tails, but in some the tail is *very* short and not a very noticeable feature.

Among the longer-tailed partridges, in which the tail is more than half the length of the closed wing, we find the Snow-cocks, the Snow-partridge, the Bamboo-partridge, the Spur-fowls, the Chukor, the Tibetan partridge, and the Francolins. Of these :—

The *Snow-cocks* (two species) are easily distinguished by their great size, being a foot and-a-half long, and bulkier than an ordinary fowl. No other Indian partridge exceeds fifteen inches.

The *Snow-partridge* is at once recognisable by having the front of the shanks feathered half-way down, the only other Indian game bird with this peculiarity being the very easily distinguishable Monauls.

The *Bamboo-partridge* has a particularly long tail, only about an inch shorter than the wing.

The *Spur-fowls* (three species) have equally long tails, but their eyes are surrounded by a bare skin, unlike those of the Bamboo-partridges.

The *Chukor* is easily recognisable by its plain drab upper surface.

The *Tibetan partridge* by the black patch in the middle of its breast.

The *Francolins* (five species) include all the other medium-tailed partridges. They may be known by having no striking points, so to speak; no particular length of tail, no bare skin round the eye or feathering on the shanks; their backs are never plain drab, nor have they a conspicuous black patch on the breast.

To the section of partridges with *very* short tails belong the hill partridges, the Green-legged partridge, the chestnut Wood-partridge, the Crested partridge and the Seesee, distinguished as follows :—

The *Hill partridges* (six species) by their remarkably long nails.

The *Green-legged partridge* by a peculiar patch of white downy feathers under the wing, just behind the armpit.

The *Chestnut Wood-partridge* by being mostly of a chestnut colour.

The *Crested partridge* by the male being dark blue and the female green.

The *Seesee* by its sandy colour and pale yellow legs.

In the present chapter I propose to deal briefly with the Alpine Snow-cocks and Snow-partridge, the Chukor, and the desert-haunting Seesee.

The Snow-cocks are very large grey birds, living on the mountains above the forest-level, and feeding on grass chiefly—there is not much else to eat where they are found. Two species are found with us. The cocks and hens are alike in plumage, but the former alone are spurred.

The Himalayan Snow-cock.

Tetraogallus himalayensis, Faun. Brit. Ind., Birds, Vol. IV, p. 143.

NATIVE NAMES :—*Kullu*, *Lupu*, *Baera*, in Western Nepal ; *Huinwal*, in Kumaun ; *Jermonal*, in the hills north of Mussoorie ; *Leepin*, Kulu ; *Golound*, in Chamba ; *Gourkagu* or *Kubuk*, in Kashmir ; *Kabk-i-dara*, in Afghanistan. The name *Ram-chukor* is, I believe, used in Gilgit. It is really the best one for these birds, which are really gigantic relatives of the Chukor.

The general colour of this bird is grizzled grey with some chestnut markings ; the throat is white with a chestnut border and the breast white with some black bars; the pinion-quills are white with broad black tips. The bill is horn colour, the feet orange, and the eyes dark, with a patch of bare yellow skin behind them. The hen is easily distinguishable from the cock by her much smaller size; she is about two inches under two feet long, while he exceeds that length by about two inches. Young birds show some brown mottling on the forehead which is not present in old ones.

This noble partridge is found from Afghanistan and Central Asia all along the Himalayas as far as Kumaon. According to season it is found at from 18,000 to 7,000 feet elevation, keeping usually in flocks, which frequent open rocky ground. It breeds high up, from May to July, usually laying five eggs, drab with reddish brown spots, and reaching nearly three inches in length. The golden eagle appears to spend a good deal of its time in trying to catch these birds, without very much success; for they are very wideawake, and the human hunter finds a rifle the best weapon with which to come to terms with them. And then when they are brought to bag they are not good eating according to European tastes, although natives are glad enough to get them. The call of this bird is a whistle which it keeps uttering all the while it flies.

The Tibetan Snow-cock.

Tetraogallus tibetanus, Faun. Brit. Ind., Birds, Vol. IV, page 144.

NATIVE NAME :—*Hrak-pa*, Bhutia in Sikkim.

This bird bears a general resemblance to the last, but is considerably smaller; it has no chestnut about the neck, and the breast is devoid of black markings, but crossed by a broad grey band. The most striking differences, however, are that the under-parts are streaked with black and white instead of being grey, and that the pinion-quills are brown with white tips. The cock and hen do not differ much in size in this species, and even the former is smaller than the hen of the Himalayan bird. The cock's bill and legs are red, and there is a red skin round the dark eyes. The hen's bill, however, is of a greenish colour, though she appears not to differ in plumage. Young birds, however, have only the throat white, the breast being grizzled with dark-grey and buff, and Mr. Ogilvie-Grant, our leading authority on Game-birds, is disposed to think that the so-called *T. henrici* is simply a young *tibetanus*.

This species is properly a Tibetan bird, but in our territory it has been found in Ladak, Spiti, Kumaun and Sikkim, always at a very high elevation, being an even more alpine bird than the last. All that is known about its breeding is that its egg is like that of the Himalayan species, but smaller. It appears to be a much better bird for the table.

Three other species of this genus inhabit mountain-ranges outside India.

Altai Snow-cock.

Tetraogallus altaicus, Brit. Mus. Cat., Birds, Vol. XXII, p. 110.

The Snow-cock of the Altai is most like the Tibetan, but has a black bill and some white at the base of the outer pinion-quills.

Caspian Snow-cock.

Tetraogallus caspicus, Brit. Mus. Cat., Birds, Vol. XXII, p. 108.

This is like the Himalayan Snow-cock, but has no chestnut about the back of the neck, a grey breast, and is paler generally. It inhabits the mountains from the Caucasus to South Persia.

Caucasian Snow-cock.

Tetraogallus caucasicus, Brit. Mus. Cat., Birds, Vol. XXII, p. 109.

This species, found on the highest parts of the Caucasus, is distinguished from the Caspian species by the chestnut patch at the back of the head, and by the grey of the upper back and breast being mixed with buff.

The Grouse-Pheasants (*Tetraophasis*) are big birds of the size and shape of Monauls, but plainly coloured, with no sex difference except the presence of spurs in the male.

The Dark-throated Grouse-Pheasant.

Tetraophasis obscurus, Brit. Mus. Cat., Birds, Vol. XXII, p. 102.

Ranges from East Tibet to the Kansu mountains ; colour dull brown and grey, with outer tail-feathers tipped first black and then white ; throat chestnut.

The Pale-throated Grouse-Pheasant.

Tetraophasis szchenyii, Brit. Mus. Cat., Birds, Vol. XXII, p. 103.

Distinguished from the above by the fawn-coloured throat and greyer lower back ; found in the Central Tibetan Mountains.

The Snow-Partridge.

Lerwa nivicola, Faun. Brit. Ind., Birds, Vol. IV, page 145.

NATIVE NAMES :—*Lerwa*, Bhutia; *Janguria*, Kumaun; *Quoir monal*, Garhwal; *Golabi*, *Bhair*, *Ter Titar*, Bashahr, etc.; *Barf ka Titar*, Kulu; *Biju*, Chamba.

This is a much smaller bird than the Snow-cocks, and in appearance and habits much recalls a Ptarmigan. The cock and hen are alike in plumage, but the former is distinguished by possessing spurs.

The head, neck and upper plumage generally are closely barred with black and white, the latter colour running into buff in places; the under-parts are mostly of a dark chestnut. This rich plumage is well set off by the red beak and legs. The eyes are dark. Young birds are less distinctly barred and are mottled with black below. The length is about fifteen inches, with a wing of nearly eight, tail four-and-a-half, bill nearly one, and shank half an inch longer.

The Snow-partridge inhabits the Himalayas from Kashmir to Sikkim and extends to Moupin and Western China. It is locally distributed with us, and is usually found at very high elevations, close up to the snow, among stones and stunted herbage. Its usual elevation is about 11,000 feet, though in winter it may come down as low as 7,000. It goes in pairs in the breeding season, and its chicks have been found late in June. Later on it is found in coveys, and affords excellent sport; it is also remarkably good to eat. But as it is commonly found on the same ground as Burrhel and Tahr, it is usually neglected by sportsmen for the nobler game.

The Tibetan Partridge.

Perdix hodgsoniæ, Faun. Brit. Ind., Birds, Vol. IV, p. 142.

NATIVE NAME :—*Sakpha,* Tibetan.

This partridge bears a strong resemblance to the common partridge at home; the cock and hen are alike, and neither of them possesses spurs. The plumage is an intricate mixture of buff, black and chestnut, with the throat white and neck chestnut; the under-parts are white, barred with black, which colour forms a patch in the centre, and there is a black patch on each cheek; the bill and legs are of a dirty green, and there is some reddish skin round the eye.

This bird is about a foot long, with a wing of six inches.

The species is, properly speaking, a native of Tibet, but it has strayed into our territories, one having been got by Mr. Wilson in the Bhagirathi valley, when shooting chukor in the autumn of 1841. It appears to be a bird of very high elevations. Its eggs have been taken in Tibet in July; they were ten in number, and of a pale drab tint without spots.

Prjevalsky's Partridge.

Perdix sifanica, Brit. Mus. Cat., Birds, Vol. XXII, p. 195.

Very like the Tibetan partridge, this species, from Kansu, may be distinguished by having no black patch on the breast, and by the admixture of chestnut in the black cheek patch, which is also smaller; the bird is smaller altogether than the Tibetan.

Copyright. L. Medland.

CHUKOR.

Copyright. L. Medland.

BLACK PARTRIDGE, COCK.

The Common European Partridge.

Perdix perdix, Brit. Mus. Cat., Birds, Vol. XXII, p. 187.

This familiar bird is of a finely pencilled brown and buff above, and finely pencilled grey on the breast, with the head buff, and a chestnut patch below the breast; the hen has this when young, and then is best distinguished by having a patch on the flat of the wing barred across with buff as well as streaked with this colour, the cock only having the central streaks. In addition to Europe, this partridge inhabits Western Asia east to North Persia; it has been introduced also into the United States.

Bearded Partridge.

Perdix daurica, Brit. Mus. Cat., Birds, Vol. XXII, p. 193.

This Partridge differs from the common species by having the throat feathers long and pointed, and the buff of this region extending right down the breast; the "horse-shoe" mark below this is black, not chestnut. The hen has less buff and black on the breast. This species ranges from Central Asia to North China; it is often exported frozen, and may be seen in the London shops.

The Chukor.

Caccabis chucar, Faun. Brit. Ind., Birds, Vol. IV, p. 131.

NATIVE NAMES :—*Chukar*, Hindi; *Kabk*, Persian; *Kau-kau*, Kashmir; *Chukru*, Chamba.

The chukor is one of the group of red-legged partridges to which the well-known "French partridge" (*Caccabis rufa*) belongs, and much resembles that bird. The cock and hen are alike in plumage, but the former may be distinguished by having a knob or blunt spur on each leg.

The plumage above and on the breast is of a plain grey without any markings, with a tinge of reddish in places and sometimes verging on olive-brown; the throat is white or buff, surrounded by a black band. The lower parts below the breast are buff, and the flanks very beautifully banded vertically with grey, buff, black and chestnut. The bill, legs and eyelids are red, and the eyes themselves dark or orange.

The cock, which is a little larger than the hen, is about fifteen inches long, with the wing six inches and-a-half, tail just over four, shank nearly two, and bill just over one.

The chukor has a very wide range, from Greece to China. It is a lover of open hilly ground, and with us is found on the Himalayas, in the hilly parts of the Punjab and in the higher hills of Sind west of the Indus. According to the country it inhabits, it is found from the sea-level up to 12,000 feet, and in Tibet even to 16,000. Himalayan birds are darker and browner in tint, but in Ladak, the Western Punjab, and Sind—in dry open tracts, in fact—are paler and greyer. The birds haunt open hill-sides among grass and scattered bushes, but may also be found in more or less wooded country and in cultivation. In winter they go in coveys or even flocks, but in the breeding season in pairs. The said season is from April to August, varying according to the elevation; for birds at high levels of course breed later. The eggs are up to a dozen, cream-colour with brown or lilac spots. The chukor is a noisy bird, and its two-syllabled note has given origin to its name. It is a fairly good sporting bird, but not so good to eat as some other partridges. The ancient

Greeks, judging from a passage in Xenophon, appear to have been in the habit of riding it down, a sport which is still practised in Yarkand.

The chukor is a good bird for introduction abroad where partridges are required, on account of its adaptable contstitution. It was tried in New Zealand, and bade fair to succeed, but the birds were not sufficiently protected, and were all shot off almost at once. It would hardly be worth while to turn it out in England, as we have already the very similar red-legged partridge there. Indeed, I have been asked whether the two were not identical. But the red-leg or "Frenchman" at home is a brown-backed bird, not greyish, and has a number of black spots bordering the black necklace outside, and thus is easily distinguishable from the chukor.

Prjevalsky's Chukor.

Caccabis magna, Brit. Mus. Cat., Birds, Vol. XXII, p. 120.

This is larger than the common chukor, and has the black throat-band bordered with chestnut ; the general colour is paler. Moreover, it is a more silent bird, though occasionally uttering a two-syllabled note of a hollow sound, peculiar to itself. It inhabits South Kokonor, Tibet, and Tsaidam.

Black-headed Chukor.

Caccabis melanocephala, Brit. Mus. Cat., Birds, Vol. XXII, p. 122.

Much the largest of the chukor genus, being as big as a hen pheasant, this species is likewise distinguished by its black cap and very grey colour. It is found in South-West Arabia, and is common in the country inland of Aden.

The Seesee.

Ammoperdix bonhami, Faun. Brit. Ind., Birds, Vol. IV, p. 133.

NATIVE NAMES :—*Sisi*, Punjab and Sind; *Tihu*, Persian.

This is a short-tailed little desert partridge, with plumage beautifully adapted for concealing it in its natural haunts. The cock and hen differed somewhat in colour, but neither has any spurs.

The cock is of a grizzled sandy hue above with a grey head and fore-neck, and the under-parts below this pinky buff. There is a black streak along each side of the head with a white one under it, and the flanks are streaked with black and chestnut.

The hen has no black and white markings on the head nor chestnut on the flanks; the lower plumage is barred with brown and buff.

The bill is orange, the eyes yellow or brown, and the legs yellow. The cock, which is rather larger than the hen, is ten inches long, with a wing of five-and-a-half.

The Seesee inhabits hilly deserts, avoiding cover, though it may be found on grassy slopes. In India it inhabits the Salt Range and Khariar Hills in the Punjab, Hazara, and all the Sind and Punjab ranges west of the Indus. It is also found in Baluchistan, Afghanistan and Persia; and has been reported from Aden.

It has a soft clear double note, recalling its name; and is not usually gregarious, though small coveys may be found in winter.

The breeding season is from April to June, and as with the chukor, the eggs may be as many as twelve in number, but they are creamy-white in colour without any spots.

Hey's Seesee.

Ammoperdix heyi, Brit. Mus. Cat., Birds, Vol. XXII, p. 125.

Hardly more than a race of the Indian Seesee, this bird is distinguished by having no black band on the head, and some chestnut on the cheek; the hens are alike. The species inhabits the countries bordering the Red Sea, and ranges to Palestine, Egypt, and the Persian Gulf.

CHAPTER VII.

Francolins and Spur-fowl.

The partridge to which the above names are applied form two very distinct groups, the Spur-fowl in particular being very easily recognisable. They are smallish birds, quite partridges in size, but with longer tails than partridges usually have; and as they sometimes raise these in a folded form, they remind one much at times of small bantam fowls, their resemblance to these being increased by the bare red skin which, as in fowls, surrounds their eyes. The cocks are always quite different in plumage from the hens, and have two or three spurs on each leg, the hens having one, two, or none.

These birds are perhaps just as much miniature jungle-fowl as partridges, but as they have not the hackles or long tail of the jungle-cocks, they may as well be classed with the partridges as anywhere else, the various groups of the pheasant family being inter-related in such a complex way that it is quite impossible to arrange them naturally in a line so to speak—a difficulty which besets all classifications.

The Spur-fowl are only found in India and Ceylon, three species being known; they all keep much to cover and are difficult to flush.

The Red Spur-fowl.

Galloperdix spadicea, Faun. Brit. Ind., Birds, Vol. IV, p. 106.

NATIVE NAMES:—*Chota jungli murghi*, Hind. in Central Provinces; *chakrotri*, *kokatri*, Mahrattas in the Syhadri Range; *kustoor*, Mahrattas of the Deccan; *sarrava koli*, Tamil; *yerra-kodi*, *jitta kodi*, Telugu.

The general colour of the male of this species is chestnut, the female being mottled black and buff; the legs and base of the bill are red, as well as the naked skin round the eyes. The cock is about fourteen inches long, with a six-inch tail, and wing exceeding this by half-an-inch, the bill from gape is an inch in length, and the shank nearly twice this. The hen is a little smaller.

This Spur-fowl inhabits the base of the Himalayas in Oudh, and is found in the Peninsula South of the Indo-Gangetic plain wherever the locality is suitable, for it avoids cultivation and open country, frequently hilly forest land.

It varies a good deal in plumage, birds from Mount Abu and the neighbourhood being paler, especially the hens, in which the black pencilling on the back is very scanty, and the ground-colour pale and greyish. About Matheran and Mahableshwar, also, hen birds are very lightly pencilled, although the ground-colour is as rich as in typical specimens.

This bird is shy and often solitary, a great runner, and seldom seen on the wing; the call of the male is said to be well imitated by the Mahratta name *kokatri*, being a kind of crow; the general note is a harsh cackle. It breeds between February and June, and possibly again towards the end of the year; three to seven eggs are laid, of a buff or greyish colour. It is good eating in the cold weather, but requires hanging for a few days.

The Painted Spur-fowl.

Galloperdix lunulata, Faun. Brit. Ind., Birds, Vol. IV, p. 108.

NATIVE NAMES :—*Kaingir*, Uriya ; *Askal*, Orissa and Singbhum ; *Hutka*, Gond in Chamba ; *Kul-koli*, Tamil ; *Jitta-kodi*, Telugu.

This bird is slightly smaller than the last, the male being little over a foot in length ; it also shows very little red round the eye. Its colour, however, makes it easily distinguishable from any other partridge like bird. The general hue is chestnut, with white black-edged spots ; the head is speckled with black and white, the crown being glossed with green ; the shoulders are also dark glossy green, and the tail is green-black, and the breast buff with black spots.

The hen is of a uniform sooty brown, with the head mostly chestnut. The bill and feet are dusky in both sexes, not red as in the other species.

This beautifully-marked bird especially affects rocky hills, and is somewhat locally distributed. It appears not to occur at all on the Malabar coast, nor in North-Western India, nor is it found in the

Bombay Presidency, north of Belgaum, nor anywhere north of the Ganges. Although it occurs in some parts of the Red Spur-fowl's territory, it does not extend so far to the west or north. Its breeding-season is from March to May, and the eggs, which are glossy and pale drab in colour, do not exceed five in number.

The Ceylon Spur-fowl.

Galloperdix bicalcarata, Faun. Brit. Ind., Birds, Vol. IV. p. 109.

NATIVE NAMES :—*Haban* or *Saban-kukula*.

In size this bird is intermediate between the last two, but has a shorter tail than either of them. The cock has a speckled appearance, being streaked above and on the flanks with white on a black ground; the neck in front is white with black edgings, and the breast pure white; the rump is chestnut, and there is an intermixture of this colour on the shoulders; the tail and most of the wings are black, and the lower part of the belly dark brown with pale spots.

The hen is of a dull chestnut brown, and both sexes have red bills and feet as well as a red bare space round the eye.

This is the only Spur-fowl found in Ceylon, and it is confined to that island. Even there its range is not universal, for it is absent from the dry northern portion. Being like the rest of the group, an inveterate skulker, and having a cackling note, it is more often heard than seen. It breeds from April to August, the eggs being cream-coloured and usually only four in number.

The Francolins are a numerous group of partridges, mostly found in Africa; five species are, however, Indian, and these include the most widely spread and best known of our partridges. They are of the typical partridge form, with tails of medium length, and no bare skin about the eyes. In all, the cocks differ from the hens either in plumage or by possessing spurs; these are always absent in the hens. The Francolins are inclined to affect cultivation, and are the best of our partridges for sporting purposes.

The commonest of all is—

The Grey Partridge.

Francolinus pondicerianus, Faun. Brit. Ind., Birds, Vol. IV, p. 139.

NATIVE NAMES:—*Titar*, *Ram titar*, *gora titar*, *safed titar*, Hind.; *Khyr*, Bengali, Uriya; *Gowjal huki*, Canarese; *Kondari*, Tamil; *Kaweenju*, Telugu; *Oussa-watuwa*, Cingalese.

The sexes are alike in colour in this species; the upper parts are brown, boldly pencilled with dark-edged creamy-white bars, and the lower parts buff with fine dark transverse pencilling; the throat is buff surrounded by a broken blackish band, and the outer tail-feathers chestnut. The bill is dark grey, the eyes dark, and the legs dull red. The cock is distinguished from the hen by being slightly larger and by having a sharp spur on each leg; he is just over a foot long, with the wing nearly six inches, and the shank about an inch and a half.

This bird is found almost all over India, but it avoids swamps and thick forest, and does not usually ascend hills to a higher level than 1,500 feet. It is absent from Lower Bengal and from the Malabar coast south of Bombay, and it is not found east of India; westwards, however, it ranges as far as the Persian Gulf.

It is most abundant where cultivation is interspersed with bush jungle, and its harsh shrill call, beginning with single notes, and continued in tri-syllables, is familiar to everyone, for it is as well known in towns as in the country, being a favourite cage-bird with the natives. Some of them like the note, but the great reason for keeping partridges is the sport they afford as fighting birds. So pugnacious are they, that I have seen two birds let out of their cages near a lawn which had no idea of "going to grass," but flew at each other straightway; and they are commonly caught by putting out a tame cock on a cage garnished with nooses, in which his wild assailants are caught. To make him call and challenge them, he is blown upon, an act which excites him to the greatest fury. Many birds also, at Calcutta at any rate, are brought in as mere chicks, and reared by hand. It may be that such specimens are the very tame ones one sees following their owners like so many little dogs, when let out; but possibly this partridge, like the chukor, can easily be tamed when adult. Double-spurred birds now and then occur, and are naturally preferred by the natives for fighting, but I have never seen such an one.

For ordinary sporting purposes, amongst Europeans, this partridge is not much esteemed; it is hard to flush, being an inveterate runner, and when you have got it is apt to be dry and flavourless; the best time to get it in good condition is in the early part of the cold weather. It has a very bad reputation as a filthy feeder, but both Pea-fowl and Jungle-fowl, when found near villages, are by no means blameless in this respect, so that very possibly the humble partridge is not so very much behind his betters.

The breeding-season of this bird is an extended one, for while it usually goes to nest between February and June, many breed a second time between September and November; the eggs are brownish white, and six to nine form the set.

The Swamp Partridge.

Francolinus gularis, Faun. Brit. Ind., Birds, Vol. IV, p. 141.

NATIVE NAMES:—*Khyah*, *Khyr*, *Kaijah*, Bengali; *Koi*, *koera*, Assamese; *Bhil-titar*, Cachari; it was formerly sometimes erroneously called *Chukore* by European sportsmen.

This species is easily distinguished from most of our partridges by its large size and comparatively long legs; as in the last species, the sexes are alike in plumage, but the cock is easily distinguishable by his spurs. The upper plumage is brown barred with buff, and the outer tail-feathers chestnut, as in the Grey Partridge; but the throat is bright rust-red, and the rest of the under-parts brown longitudinally streaked with white. The bill is blackish, the eyes dark, and the feet dull red.

The cock of this species, which is a little larger than the hen, will measure fifteen inches, though his tail is only a little over four; the wing is more than seven inches, and the shank two and-a-quarter.

The Swamp Partridge, as its name implies, has a habitat quite different from our other species, affecting high grass and cane-brakes near the edges of rivers and jheels, though it will come into cultivated ground to feed. It haunts the alluvial plains of the Ganges and Brahmaputra, extending from Pilibhit to the extremity of Assam and Cachar, and even occurs occasionally on the Khasi plateau; but it is not found in the Sundarbans. Very little is known about its breeding, but on two occasions five eggs of the species have been taken in April; they were cream-coloured and slightly speckled.

Owing to the localities which it frequents, the Swamp Partridge is usually shot from elephants; but Blanford states that he has shot it on foot near Colgong, in grass only three or four feet high. He says it much resembles the common Grey Partridge in its edible qualities, as it also does in its call; and it is equally pugnacious. Mr. Hume, in the "Game-birds of India," falls foul of his artist for representing this species standing in water like a wading-bird. No doubt the draughtsman represented it thus in ignorance, but it would be interesting to know if this, one of the very few swamp-haunting birds in the pheasant family, ever does voluntarily go into water in the wild state. The keeper of the aviary in which a specimen of this species was confined in the London Zoo told me that he had seen it standing in water.

The Black Partridge.

Francolinus vulgaris, Faun. Brit. Ind., Birds, Vol. IV, p. 135.

NATIVE NAMES :—*Kala-titar*, Hind. ; *Kais-titar* (the female) Nepal; *Tetra*, Garhwal ; *Vrembi* of the Manipuris.

In this species the cock is spurred, and his plumage differs conspicuously from that of the female. His general colour is black, with a long white patch on each side of the face, large white spots along the flanks, and close white barring on the lower part of the back and the tail. There is a chestnut collar round the neck, and a patch of the same colour under the tail; the shoulders and most of the wings are brown marked with buff, the markings following the edge of the feathers; the quills are barred with buff. The belly is pale chestnut marked with white ; the crown streaked light and dark brown.

The hen is somewhat like the cock above, but the barring of the back and tail is coarser, and brown and buff instead of black and white. She shows no black on the head or below, and no chestnut on the neck except at the back of it. She has the eyebrows and sides of the head buff, the throat nearly white, and the rest of the lower parts buff irregularly pencilled with brown.

Young cocks are more spotted with white than the old birds, and young hens also are spotted on the breast, not pencilled like old ones.

The bill is black in the cock and dark brown in the hen; the eyes dark and the legs orange-red in both sexes.

The sexes both vary in size, but the cocks are the largest; one will measure about thirteen and-a-half inches, with the tail four inches and the wing just over six; the shank is about two.

The Black Partridge with us inhabits Northern India from Sind to Manipur; its Southern boundary runs south of Cutch and north of Kattywar, and thence to the Chilka lake in Orissa. To the northward it ascends the outer slopes of the Himalayas, following the river valleys, to about 5,000 feet; Manipur is its eastern and southern limit, but it has a wide range to the west of India, ranging through Persia and Asia Minor even to Cyprus. It formerly inhabited Greece, Italy, Sicily, and Spain, and appear to have been the bird known to the Greeks and Romans as *Attagen*, and much esteemed for the table. It has, however, become extinct in these western countries, and is evidently a bird which needs careful preservation. This it well deserves, as it is an excellent sporting bird, and very good eating; in fact, it is one of the most desirable of all partridges. Its stronghold in India is the Indo-Gangetic plain and the regions adjacent; it especially frequents high grass and tamarisk scrub near water and cultivation, and often cultivated ground itself. It is generally met with singly or in pairs. The male has a terribly harsh call-note or crow, which he is fond of uttering from an ant-hill. There is a pretty native legend which renders the call as "*Subhan, teri kudrat*," but I have never been able to fit these pious words to it, or any others. The Black Partridge breeds from May to August, most birds nesting in June; the eggs are fairly numerous, six to ten, and drab in colour.

The Painted Partridge or Francolin.

Francolinus pictus, Faun. Brit. Ind., Birds, Vol. IV, p. 137.

NATIVE NAMES :—*Titar, kala titar*, Mahratta; *Kakhera kodi*, Telugu.

In this species neither sex possesses spurs, and the cock and hen are much alike, though not indistinguishable. It is rather smaller than the Black Partridge. The cock is not unlike the male Black Partridge, above, but very different below, being so heavily spotted with white that there is only enough black to separate the spots; there is no chestnut collar round the neck, but the eyebrows, face, and throat are chestnut. In the hen the throat is whitish, and the bars on the back are buff, and wider apart than in the cock. The bill is blackish, the eyes dark, and the legs orange-red.

This bird occupies a territory south of the Black Partridges, the southern limit of that bird being the northern frontier of the painted species; this becomes rarer towards the south, and is absent from the Malabar Coast, south of Bombay, as also from Mysore. Nor is it found in the Peninsula, south of Coimbatore, although occurring in Ceylon on some of the hills west and south of Newera

Eliya. It is not found east or west of India. It meets the Black Partridge on the boundary of that species, and hybrids between the two are occasionally found. Its general habits and qualifications as a sporting bird and table delicacy are much the same as those of the Black Partridge, and it may be regarded as one of our most desirable Game-birds. It is more often found in cultivated land than the other species, and also more frequently occurs in dry grass land at a distance from water, so that it would appear to be of a more adaptable nature. Another detail of its habits which differs from those of the other species is its partiality for perching in trees, whence the male frequently calls; he has a different and less harsh note. The nest and eggs are much like those of the Black Partridge, but the present bird seems to breed somewhat later.

The Eastern or Chinese Francolin.

Francolinus chinensis, Faun. Brit. Ind., Birds, Vol. IV, p. 138.

NATIVE NAME :—*Kha*, Burmese.

The Chinese Francolin is intermediate in size between the black and the painted Francolins; the sexes differ in colour nearly as conspicuously as those of the black species, and the male alone possesses spurs. His general colour is black, spotted with white, the spots becoming broad bars on the belly. The top of the head is brown with pale edges and black forehead and eyebrows; there is another black band from the corner of the mouth to below the ears, and between this and the eyebrow a white streak covers the side of the face, the throat also being white. The lower back is black with close narrow white bars; under the tail is a chestnut patch, and the shoulder-feathers and innermost wing—quills are edged with chestnut and have the spots buff.

The hen is brown above, with a pale mottling; the lower back is barred with buff and brown; the chin and throat dirty white, and the under-parts below this buff barred with dark brown, and plain chestnut under the tail. On the head the eyebrows and cheek-stripes are brown and the light band buff.

The beak is dark brown, eyes light hazel, and legs orange.

This Francolin is found, in our Indian empire, only in certain parts of Burma and in Karennee. It is common in certain localities, north of Prome, in the Irrawaddy valley, and has also been obtained in Toungoo and the Thoungyen valley. Outside Burma it inhabits South China, Cochin China and Siam. Its general habits resemble those of the two previous species; it haunts forest clearings and waste land, and is also found in bamboo jungle. In Burma it breeds in June and July; as many as eight eggs may be laid, and they are pale buff in colour.

Large-billed Francolin.

Rhizothera longirostris, Brit. Mus. Cat., Birds, Vol. XXII, p. 183.

This peculiar Partridge, which ranges from the south of the Malay Peninsula to Borneo, is at once recognisable by its large bill, which is big enough for a Peacock, though the bird is of the ordinary Partridge size, about fourteen inches long. Both sexes are spurred. The cock is mottled with brown, black, and buff above, mixed with grey on the lower back; the face and the back are chestnut, the neck and breast grey, the abdomen deep buff; the hen has less grey on the back and a chestnut breast.

Hose's Large-billed Francolin.

Rhizothera dulitensis, OGILVIE GRANT, Game-birds, Vol. I, p. 142.

This race, from Mount Dalit, in Borneo, has the grey extending further down the breast in the male, and the abdomen white. The hen is richer and darker in tint than that of *longirostris*.

CHAPTER VIII.

The Forest Partridge.

The Partridges which remain to be dealt with are pre-eminently forest birds, never going far from cover, and often perching. Most of them have very short tails, but one, the Bamboo Partridge, has the tail longer than in any other Indian species, so as rather to recall a small pheasant in appearance.

The Bamboo Partridge.

Bambusicola fytchii, Faun. Brit. Ind., Birds, Vol. IV, p. 110.

This Partridge shows no difference in plumage according to sex ; the male has a spur on each shank, but this may be present in the female also. The plumage is brown above, spotted with chestnut for the most part ; the face is buff, with a dark band behind the eye ; the breast dull chestnut with some white spots, and the under-parts below this buff, with large black spots shaped like a heart. The tail is barred brown and buff, and the pinion quills are chestnut without bars. The bill is brown, the eyes orange-hazel, and the legs grey.

This Partridge is about fourteen inches long, of which the tail measures nearly five ; thus, it is easy to distinguish it from any other species, the Spur-fowl, which also have longish tails, showing some bare skin about the eye.

The Bamboo Partridge affects forest and high grass, and ranges through a considerable portion of the eastern hill tracts, from the Assam hills south of the Brahmaputra, through Manipur, to the Kachyeng hills between Upper Burma and Yunnan. It is shy and has a loud harsh call. Although the time—May and June—of breeding appears to be known, the eggs are as yet desiderata.

Chinese Bamboo Partridge.

Bambusicola thoracica, Brit. Mus. Cat., Birds, Vol. XXII, p. 258.

This species, confined to South China, is mottled above with brown, chestnut, and buff; the face, throat and tail are chestnut; the eyebrows and chest grey, and the rest of the under-parts buff spotted with black at the sides.

Formosan Bamboo Partridge.

Bambusicola sonorivox, Brit. Mus. Cat., Birds, Vol. XXII, p. 258.

This, the Formosan representative of the last species, differs by having the sides of the face grey as well as the eyebrows, and being darker generally. Its eggs are light brown in colour.

The various Hill-Partridges (*Arboricola*) form an easily recognizable group of short-tailed birds with rather long spurless shanks, and particularly long, nearly-straight claws. The sexes are usually alike, and they inhabit hill forests, keeping very close to cover, and occasionally perching. They are seldom if ever seen, and little is known about their breeding, except that they lay half-a-dozen or more white eggs on the ground. Their call is a low soft whistle, and they are unobtrusive birds altogether; yet they are a well represented group with us, numbering no less than six species, none of which, however, are found in Southern India or Ceylon. An interesting point about these partridges is that they possess a row of small separate bones along the upper edge of the orbit, a sort of bony eyebrow in fact. No other bird of this family possesses them, although they occur in some other groups, the Trumpeters (*Psophiidæ*) of South America and the partridge-like Tinamous (*Tinamidæ*) of the same continent. The general plan of colouration of the Indian *Arboricolas* is very similar, all having olive-brown backs, mottled with black, and grey flanks boldly spotted with white, and usually with chestnut edgings.

The Common Hill-Partridge.

Arboricola torqueola, Fauna Brit. Ind., Birds, Vol. IV, p. 125.

NATIVE NAMES :—*Peura*, *Ban-titar*, Hindi, of Kumaun and Nepal; *Roli*, *Ram chukru*, in Chamba; *Kaindal*, Kangra; *Kohum-pho*, Lepcha.

This is the only species of *Arboricola* in which the sexes are different. The male has the head bright-chestnut above and of a paler shade of the same colour over and behind the ear coverts; the eyebrows, sides of the head, and throat are black, with white edgings at the sides, and there is a white moustache-streak. The breast is grey, separated from the black throat by a white band. The skin surrounding the eye is scarlet.

In the hen the crown is brown with black streaks, the sides of the head and the throat are chestnut with black spots; the breast is brownish, and has a rusty band above it; and the white spots on the flanks tend to run up to the breast, and are larger. However, old hens lose the breast spots, and young cocks possess them. Hens and young cocks have the skin round the face purplish-red. In all, the bill is black and the legs flesh-grey.

This partridge is a little under a foot long, with a tail of only three inches, and a shank nearly two. The wing is six inches long. Males run larger than females.

The common hill-partridge is found at moderate elevations along the Himalayas from Chamba to east of Sikkim, and also in the Naga hills and in those north of Manipur. It ranges from 5,000 to 14,000 feet, but its common range does not go above 9,000. South of Manipur it is replaced by a race (*A. batemani*) with the chestnut and black band from the ear-coverts extending all down the sides of the neck instead of half-way.

Blyth's Hill-Partridge.

Arboricola rufigularis, Fauna Brit. Ind., Birds, Vol. IV, p. 126.

NATIVE NAMES:—In Kumaun and among the Lepchas this species seems to have the same names as the last; in the Daphla hills it is called *Pokhu*.

This species, like those which follow, appears to be a little smaller than the last.

It has the crown olive-brown with black streaks, and the eyebrows and face white, mostly speckled with black. The throat is chestnut with black spots, and below this is a band of plain chestnut, generally divided from the grey breast by a black band. The pure grey of the breast and the absence of black bars on the back will distinguish this bird from the hen of the Common Hill-Partridge.

The beak is black, the skin round the eyes dull dark-red, and the legs red.

This also is a Himalayan bird, ranging from Kumaun to the Daphla hills, but inhabiting lower elevations than the Common Hill-Partridge, since it is found from the foot of the hills to 6,000 feet only. It is also found in the Karennee and Tenasserim hills, and specimens from these localities are usually without the black band dividing the red neck from the grey breast. Four eggs of a dirty white colour were taken below Darjeeling early in July.

The Arrakan Hill-Partridge.

Arboricola intermedia, Fauna Brit. Ind., Birds, Vol. IV, p. 127.

NATIVE NAME :—*Toung-kha*, Burmese.

This is hardly a distinct species, merely differing from the last in having the throat entirely black instead of being only spotted with that colour. It agrees with the eastern variety of Blyth's Hill-Partridge in having no black band across the chest.

It is found in the Arrakan hills and North Pegu, extending to North Cachar and the Naga hills, and to Eastern Manipur, where it is common. The eggs were taken in Manipur in May; they were pure white, and six in number.

The White-cheeked or Black-throated Hill-Partridge.

Arboricola atrigularis, Fauna Brit. Ind., Birds, Vol. IV, p. 127.

NATIVE NAMES:—*Peura* in Sylhet; *Duboy, Dubore*, Assamese; *San-batai*, in Chittagong.

In this species the crown is brown, running into grey in front and chestnut behind, the feathers marked with black; a double eyebrow, of grey above black, is present, and the eye is surrounded by a black patch; the cheeks are white, running into buff behind; the throat is black, becoming edged below first with white and then with grey, until it merges into the grey breast; the grey flanks have no chestnut borders to the feathers in this bird.

The bill is black, and the legs orange or lobster-red; and the reddish skin of the face shows through the feathers.

The White-cheeked Hill-Partridge extends from Assam south of the Brahmaputra into the Naga, Khasi, and Garo hills, Cachar, Sylhet, Tipperah, and Chittagong. The eggs have been taken in Sylhet on hillocks, at the foot of trees in dark and gloomy places; as many as four occurring in a nest. They are white, and measure rather over an inch in length.

The Red-breasted Hill-Partridge.

Arboricola mandellii, Fauna Brit. Ind., Birds, Vol. IV, p. 128.

In this very easily recognisable species, the head, neck, and breast are chestnut of various shades; the chin and throat being pale and uniform, separated from the darker breast by a white band bordered below by black; the sides and back of the neck are spotted with black, and the eyebrows are grey, meeting at the back of the head.

Nothing is known about the colour of the bill, feet, etc.; indeed, the species is a rare and little-studied one, which has only been obtained from the low hills of Bhootan and Sikhim; and once from the northern part of the Goalpara district. However, it is so distinct from all the rest that it ought to be easily identified if met with.

The Brown-breasted Hill-Partridge.

Arboricola brunneipectus, Fauna Brit. Ind., Birds, Vol. IV, p. 128.

NATIVE NAME :—Appears to be called *Toungkha*, like *A. intermedia.*

This is a very distinct form, with the face and throat buff, the latter speckled with black, the breast brownish buff, and flanks greyish buff, with the usual white spots, but no chestnut; the white-spotted feathers are tipped with black.

The bill is black, the eyelids, the skin of the throat, where this shows through the feathers, and the legs, are red, the latter varying much in intensity of colour.

This bird haunts the evergreen forests on the eastern spurs of the Pegu hills, and also inhabits the ranges east of the Sittang river as far as Tavoy, as well as the Ruby Mines District. It has not been often found, and so very little is known about it.

Fire-Necked Hill-Partridge.

Arboricola ardens, Brit. Mus. Cat., Birds, Vol. XXII, p. 210.

Known only from the Hainan mountains, this species is at once distinguished from the rest, of which it is most like the white-cheeked, by the orange-red colour of its neck and breast; only one specimen is on record.

Formosan Hill-Partridge.

Arboricola crudigularis, Brit. Mus. Cat., Birds, Vol. XXII, p. 211.

This, a Formosan mountain-bird, is distinguished from its nearest ally, the white-cheeked Tree-Partridge, by having the upper part of the throat all white and the back with bolder dark markings.

Sonnerat's Hill-Partridge.

Arboricola gingica, Brit. Mus. Cat., Birds, Vol. XXII, p. 213.

Only a single specimen of this bird has ever been obtained and that from an unknown locality more than 100 years ago; yet it is easily recognised, being distinguished by the peculiar marking on the neck, a black triangle above a narrow white band and a broad deep red one.

Rickett's Hill-Partridge.

A. ricketti, Grant, Bull. Brit. Ornith. Club, Vol. VIII, p. xlvii.

From the Kuatun hills in Foh-kien, is like it, but has a white forehead and eyebrows; very likely Sonnerat's is only a variety of this.

Javan Hill-Partridge.

Arboricola javanica, Brit. Mus. Cat., Birds, Vol. XXII, p. 214.

The Javanese mountains are the home of this species, which is grey on the back and breast, the former barred with black; the belly is chestnut, and the head also reddish brown, with black eye-stripes, and a black band down the back of the neck joining a black collar.

Red-billed Hill-Partridge.

Arboricola rubrirostris, Brit. Mus. Cat., Birds, Vol. XXII, p. 215.

A rare species, from the Sumatran mountains, with black head and neck slightly speckled with white, the breast spotted black on white, and sides barred black and white; the upper parts are barred black and brown. It is conspicuous by its red bill.

Treacher's Hill-Partridge.

Arboricola hyperythra, Brit. Mus. Cat., Birds, Vol. XXII, p. 217.

Only one specimen of this species is known, from the mountains of North-West Borneo; it is most like the Brown-breasted species, but is all chestnut below and deeper black on the crown, with the sides of the head grey.

Whitehead's Hill-Partridge.

Arboricola erythrophrys, Brit. Mus. Cat., Birds, Vol. XXII, p. 218.

This species from Mount Kina Balu in Borneo is also very similar to the Brown-breasted, but has the throat black in males, and the black cap extending down to the eyes; young birds, however, have a black-spotted brown cap and grey eyebrows, and in those in an intermediate stage the eyebrows are chestnut and the throat also.

Horsfield Hill-Partridge.

Arboricola orientalis, Brit. Mus. Cat., Birds, Vol. XXII, p. 218.

Horsfield's Tree-Partridge is dark-brown above, mottled with orange and black on the wings, with white throat and eyebrows and drab breast; the sides are mottled with grey white and black; the only specimen known came from the mountains of East Java.

Sumatran Hill-Partridge.

Arboricola sumatrana, Brit. Mus. Cat., Birds, Vol. XXII, p. 219.

This is another very rare species, inhabiting Sumatra. Its nearest ally is the last, but in the present species there are no white eyebrows, the black and white flank-markings take the form of regular bars, and the general colour above is much brighter brown, with bold black barring.

Roll's Hill-Partridge.

Arboricola rolli, Rothschild, Bull. Brit. Ornith. Club, Vol. XXV, p. 7.

Is most like the Red-billed species, but has the bill black, the crown brown, marked with black, and a large white patch on the ears. It comes from Mt. St. Bajak in N.-W. Sumatra.

Henry's Hill-Partridge.

Arboricola henrici. Oustalet, Bull. Mus. Paris, II, p. 317.

From Tonkin and Annam, is like the Brown-breasted species, but without the buff eyebrows and with the forehead chestnut instead of buff.

Campbell's Hill-Partridge.

Arboricola campbelli, Robinson, Bull. Brit. Ornith. Club, Vol. XV, p. 28.

From Tehôm Valley on the borders of Perak, most resembles the White-cheeked, but has the crown all black, and the buff on the sides of the neck replaced by white, the white spots on the flanks, on the other hand, being replaced by buff.

One partridge of this group found in our limits differs from the true *Arboricolas* in not having the peculiar bridge of bone over the eye; it is also distinguished by possessing a large patch of white downy feathers under the wing, which is ordinarily concealed, even when the wing is lifted, by the feathers of the side.

The Green-legged Hill-Partridge.

Tropicoperdix chloropus, Fauna Brit. Ind., Birds, Vol. IV, p. 129.

This bird bears a close general resemblance to the other hill-partridges, but the brown of the upper part is more closely mottled with black, and the sides of the body pale rusty with black blotches; the crown is dark-brown, the eyebrows also brown, with white streaks, and the face and throat white, speckled with blackish. Below this the front and sides of the neck are chestnut with black spots, and then the breast is coloured brown continuously with the back.

The bill is dark-red at the root and greenish at the tip; the skin round the eye purplish; and the legs pale-green.

This partridge, which agrees with the *Arboricolas* in habits as in appearance, is found, locally, in the evergreen forests all through Tenasserim down to Tavoy, and on the eastern slopes of the Pegu hills. Outside Indian limits it has been obtained in Cochin China.

Charlton's Hill-Partridge.

Tropicoperdix charltoni, Brit. Mus. Cat., Birds, Vol. XXII, p. 221.

In this species, which is found from Penang to Borneo, and is suspected of occurring in Tenasserim, the legs are red, not green; otherwise it is not unlike the last, but has even finer pencilling above regular black and buff barring on the sides, and a plain chestnut breast.

There remain two very beautiful short-tailed forest partridges, each of which claims a genus of its own.

The Chestnut Wood-Partridge.

Caloperdix oculea, Fauna Brit. Ind., Birds, Vol. IV, p. 131.

In this bird the tail, though short, is longer than in the *Arboricolas*, the toes, and especially the claws, are shorter, and the hinder toe bears a mere rudiment of a claw. The sexes are alike in plumage, but the male has short spurs, which may be one or two on each leg.

The plumage is very characteristic, the general colour being a rich chestnut, barred with black on the flanks, where also white bars may be present; the back is black, pencilled with white above and with chestnut lower down; the wings are brown with black spots, and the tail black.

The bill is black, the eyes dark, and the legs dull-green. The length is just under eleven inches, the wing being nearly six, and the tail nearly three; the shank is nearly two inches long.

This is a forest bird, very little known, and apparently one which Europeans have never even seen in the wild state. It is found in the Malay Peninsula, and extends into the southernmost part of Tenasserim, where it inhabits dense jungle about Bankasoon. A sort of local variety of the species inhabits Sumatra.

I have ventured to call this bird the "Chestnut" Partridge, as "Ferruginous," the epithet usually imposed on it, is a rare and clumsy word.

The Red-crested or Rooloo Partridge.

Rollulus roulroul, Fauna Brit. Ind., Birds, Vol. IV, p. 111.

This lovely bird very properly occupies a genus all to itself. It has a very short tail and rather long legs, with feet of the ordinary size, and the claw of the hind toe rudimentary or altogether absent. A tuft of long hair-like feathers is found on the forehead in both sexes, which otherwise differ widely, although neither has spurs.

The male, besides the tuft of bristles, has a full and large crest of loose-textured feathers on the head, which is of a dark-red colour. The general body-plumage is steel-blue with a rich satiny gloss, changing in some lights to green; the wings are brown, and there is a white band across the forehead.

The hen has no crest, and is grass-green without gloss, with chestnut wings and slate-coloured head.

In both sexes the eyelids and feet are brilliant red, the male has the base of the bill red in addition; but in the female it is all black. This bird about equals the wood-partridges in size, being about eleven inches long; the wing measures five and-a-half inches, and the tail two and-a-half; the shank about one and-a-quarter. Females are a little smaller than this.

This partridge has a wide range, being found in Borneo, Java, Sumatra, Siam, and the Malay Peninsula, where it extends into the south of Tenasserim near the Pakchan river. It is a forest bird, and gregarious in its habits, being found in small parties of half-a-dozen or more, comprising both males and females. It is described as much more lively in its movements than the *Arboricolas*, running about like a quail, and not scratching so much as the others. The note is a soft, pleasant whistle. Nothing is known about the breeding except that the egg is buff and about an inch and-a-half long. This beautiful and gentle little partridge would be a most charming aviary bird, but unfortunately it is not much exported, at any rate nowadays, and Rutledge, who imported the first into Calcutta many years ago, told me that the late ex-King of Oudh was much pleased with them and bought them at a high price, naming them "The King's Fancy." The name "Rooloo" is that by which Rutledge called these birds, and I presume it is the native name in some parts of the Far East.

Black Wood-Partridge.

Melanoperdix nigra, Brit. Mus. Cat., Birds, Vol. XXII, p. 227.

This partridge bears a general resemblance to the last but has no crest or bristles on the head, and a very thick bill. The colour is very different, the cock being all black, and the hen chestnut, variegated with black. It ranges from the Wellesley Province to Borneo.

CHAPTER IX.

Quails.

THE partridges being now disposed of, we come to the quails, under which heading, as I said in the introduction, are included all the smallest members of the pheasant family, having the closed wing under five inches in length. The term, like "teal," among the ducks, is somewhat conventional, for just as some small ducks, such as the whistlers, are called "teal," though their relationship to the proper teal is obviously small, so some of the "quails" are evidently tiny partridges rather than close allies of the typical quails. Whatever their real relationships may be, the ten little game birds which are popularly known as quails are separable as follows :—

The *Mountain quail* by having the tail well-developed, nearly as long as the closed wing ; other quails having very short tails.

The *Stout-billed Bush-quails* (2 species) by their thick, short bills, and short but well-formed tails about half as long as the wing.

The *Slight-billed Bush-quails* (4 species) by having ordinary bills and well-formed tails about two-thirds as long as the wing.

The *Typical quails* (3 species) by having no noticeable tail at all, the tail feathers being not only less than half as long as the wing, but so soft that they are not easily distinguished from the ordinary plumage of the rump.

It should be noted that the so-called Button-quails or Bustard-quails do not belong to the pheasant family at all, but form a curious little group of their own, the Hemipodes, which will be dealt with at the close of this series. They have the same soft tails as the typical quails, but differ from them and from all other *Phasionidæ* in having no hind-toe,* no web at the base of the toes, and only a single row of scales down the front of the shank. The head has also a quite different expression from that of ordinary quails, the bill being longer and the eyes yellowish white.

The typical or soft-tailed quails fall into two sections, one containing the Common, Japanese and Rain quails, with the sexes not very different and about a dozen feathers in the tail, and the other the little Painted Quail, in which the male and female are extremely unlike and there are only eight tail feathers. The plumage in these quails is marked conspicuously with light streaks above, and there is no spur in either sex, though this does not prevent the males from fighting furiously. They live always on the ground, and are more or less migratory.

---

* The Australian Plain-Wanderer (*Pedionomus torquatus*) has a hind-toe and some other Australian Hemipodes have short stout bills, but the above characters will diagnose all Indian species.

The Common Quail.

Coturnix communis, Faun. Brit. Ind., Birds, Vol. IV., p. 114.

NATIVE NAMES.—*Bater*, *Bara bater*, *Gagus bater*, Hind. ; *Batairo*, in Sind ; *Batri*, Bengali ; *Gundri*, Uriya ; *Soipol*, Manipuri ; *Botah Surrai*, Assamese ; *Bur-ganja*, *Gur-ganj*, Poona and elsewhere ; *Burli* in Belgaum ; *Gogari-Yellachi*, Telugu ; *Periaka-deh*, Tamil ; *Sipale haki*, Canarese.

Both sexes of this species are much alike, the plumage being a mixture of black, brown, and buff, streaked with cream-colour ; there is a conspicuous cream streak down the crown and eyebrow-stripes of the same colour. Below, the plumage is buff, darkening into reddish brown on the flanks, which are spotted with blackish, and boldly marked with whitish streaks. The pinion-quills are brown, with buff bars on the outer web. The bill and eyes are dark and the feet flesh-coloured.

The male has the breast without spots, and the throat dirty white with a dull black mark, shaped somewhat like an anchor, the shank running down the centre of the throat and the arms curving up on each side. The female has the throat plain whitish, but the breast is spotted with black. Although there is a good deal of variation in tint in this quail, Indian specimens are on the whole true to colour, though some males occur with a rusty ground-colour on the throat ; in Europe this, and even the marking, is more variable : and this part of the plumage may be entirely dark or rusty brown. This quail is about eight inches long, with the wing, which is longer in proportion than in any other bird in the family, four to four-and-a-half inches ; the shank is about an inch long. The hens run larger than the cocks, though the difference is not striking. The weight is between three and four ounces.

This is the most widely-spread and thoroughly migratory species of the present family ; it is found over most of Europe, Asia, and Africa, breeding in the northern parts of its range and moving southwards in winter. Great numbers are caught on migration and many must perish at sea ; I remember, many years ago, I saw one poor little thing try to board a ship I was on in the Red Sea, and, striking the side, fall into the water. Another, less utterly exhausted, was caught on board and ultimately reached the London Zoological Gardens. Most of our Empire is visited by this bird in winter, but it is most abundant in Northern India, rare in Burma, and absent from Ceylon and Tenasserim. Some come over sea on to our Western coasts—Sind, Cutch and Guzerat—but most cross the Himalayas from Central Asia, and these arrive earlier.

Their distribution with us varies with the season they encounter on reaching India. If there is plenty of food in the north, most of them stay there, but in years when the crops are deficient there, they move southward to a greater extent; moreover, in some years a great many more birds arrive than in others. In the Calcutta bazaar during the seven years I watched it, quails only came into the ordinary bird-sellers' hands one winter, 1899-1900 ; then the men had plenty of them, and they were reported as being unusually common in Bengal. Ordinarily only one man in the Calcutta bazaar had quails, and he got the birds from up-country and kept and fed them for months, being a resident and considerable dealer, unlike the men who only came in the winter to sell birds more or less locally captured.

The quails come in across the sea from the west before the end of August, and about a fortnight later the main body from the north arrive. At the end of February they begin to draw northwards again, and if the south of India has not come up to their expectations, the north will be full of them in March. Some will linger in the south for a time as others had done in the north, but in any case hardly any will stay behind permanently and breed in India.

They migrate at night as a rule, though stray specimens may be seen, at sea at any rate, by day. Mr. Hume describes how on one moonlight night in April, a few miles from Mussoorie, a huge cloud of them, "many hundred yards in length and fifty yards I suppose in breadth," passed over him quite low down. That the quail is more or less nocturnal I have little doubt. A specimen which I kept years ago in my rooms at Oxford was quite as active by night as by day, whereas ordinary birds will go to roost in a room quite irrespective of the artificial light of lamps or gas. For the same reason quails are very unsuitable inmates for a mixed aviary, unless they have a wing cut, as they will get restless at night and fly up against the roof, to the detriment not only of their own personal appearance, but also of the peace and happiness of the other inmates of the place.

A special place for quails, where these birds may be kept for food, should, however, it is said, be kept dark to prevent their fighting. The floor of a "quailery" should be well supplied with sand, and fresh turf, white ants occasionally, and a constant supply of water in a small trough should be provided in addition to their ordinary food of millet. Thus treated they will keep fat and healthy, and, as many people know, be of the greatest use in the hot weather. As they are even better to eat when properly fattened than when killed wild, it is not only humane but politic to treat them as well as possible, as is the case with all other animals in a state of captivity or domestication.

The natural food of this quail is millet and other grain when it can get it, and at other times grass-seed and small insects chiefly; it feeds chiefly in the morning and evening, resting in the middle of the day. Here and there a few pairs remain and breed with us, even in the East as far as Purneah and south in the Deccan. These, however, seem not to be of a resident strain or race, such as exists in some other countries which quail also visit as migrants, but birds which by some accident, have been unable or unwilling to depart with the rest of their kind.

Though the male has the reputation of associating with several females where the species is numerous, he appears to pair with one only in India; the nest is a mere hollow in the ground, usually with more or less of a lining of grass. In India ten eggs appear to the largest clutch, though up to fourteen may be laid in Europe.

These eggs are a little over an inch long; and are spotted with brown on a buff ground, the markings varying a good deal. They may be found in March and April. In the latter month this bird was observed to be breeding abundantly about Nowshera in 1872, which was an exceptionally backward year, so that the quail had evidently decided in many cases to make the best of things where they were and not go north, since they should have all been out of India a month later in the ordinary way.

Their haunts are in crops and the stubble of these, grass, bush jungle, any low cover in short, and they afford more good shooting than any other bird of this family in India. Their flight is low, straight and swift, and one has been seen to escape from a harrier by sheer speed; but then a harrier is not a very swift hawk. They are often very unwilling to rise, and I have been heard of one being trodden upon, which is what one might call falling a victim to a policy of *laissez-faire.*

The Japanese Quail.

Coturnix japonica, Faun. Brit. Ind., Birds, Vol. IV, p. 116.

NATIVE NAMES :—*Udzura*, Japanese; probably called *Ngon* in Burma.

This species much resembles the common grey quail, but both sexes of it have a richer chestnut tint on the flanks. This of itself would not be much to go by, but the male has the face and throat brick-red, without any trace of the dark markings found there even in the rare reddish-throated variety of the common quail; and the female is still more distinct, for although her throat is white like that of the hen of the ordinary quail, the feathers there are long and pointed instead of short and round, and the outer ones have rusty edges. The young males also possess these whiskers at first.

This quail inhabits Eastern Asia, Japan, and China. It comes at times within our limits on its winter migration, and no doubt often gets passed over as a common quail. When Mr. Oates wrote his excellent little work on the game birds of India, two specimens were in the British Museum from our Empire; both were hens, one coming from Bhutan and the other from Karennee. The latter had been procured by Major Wardlow Ramsay in 1874. Dr. Blanford, writing on the same subject in the same year (1898) as Mr. Oates, stated that he did not consider these specimens characteristic, and thought it would be better to wait till a male was recorded before including the bird as Indian. Next year, however, Lieutenant H. H. Turner shot another of the species in the Manipur Valley in February, and submitted it to me for identification with the rest of his Manipur birds. There was no doubt that this bird was a Japanese quail, as the pointed throat feathers were unmistakeable, to say nothing of the richly-coloured flanks; the specimen is now in the British Museum. Lieutenant Turner states (*Journal Asiatic Society*, 1899, p. 244) that he saw a dozen or so of the birds, which were driven out by the firing of some long grass; thinking they were only common quail, he did not trouble more about them. It would therefore be as well to examine carefully all supposed common quails shot in Burma. The ordinary species is admittedly rare there, and very possibly this one takes its place. At the same time, intermediate

Copyright. L. Medland.

RAIN-QUAIL, HEN.

Copyright. L. Medland.

WHITE-CHEEKED HILL PARTRIDGE.

specimens between the two species occur, so that it must be expected that some will turn up which cannot be fairly referred to either.

In its ordinary home this bird has the same habits as the common quail, and its eggs are similar; but the note of the male is different—a great argument for its specific distinctness. According to General Prjevalsky, this note, which alone makes this bird easily distinguishable, consists of some deep hollow sounds, several times repeated in quick succession."

The Rain-Quail or Black-breasted Quail.

Coturnix coromandelica, Faun. Brit. Ind., Birds, Vol. IV, p. 116.

NATIVE NAMES :—*Chota Batter*, Hind.; *Chanac*, Nepaul; *Kade*, Tamil; *Chinna Yellichi*, Telugu. For the most part, however, this species goes under the same names as the common quail.

This bird is very like the common quail, although a little smaller; but both sexes may be at once distinguished *by the pinion quills being plain drab*, without the pale cross-bars seen in the common species. Independently of this, the male can be distinguished by his brighter and purer colouring below. His throat-marking is pure white and jet-black, and his breast a decided warm buff, with splashes of black which increase with age till there is a decided black patch in the middle. His bill is also often of a decided black.

This quail is resident or only partially migratory, and is not known outside our Empire. Within this, however, it is very widely distributed, although it has not yet been reported from Kashmir, Tenasserim, or the Shan States; but its resemblance to the common quail no doubt often causes it to be overlooked. It has much the same habits as its larger ally, affecting grass and cultivated ground, and shifts its ground locally according to the rains, whence its name. Thus to Northern Bengal, Oudh, Behar, the North-West Provinces, the Punjab, Sind, and the open parts of Upper Burma it arrives in the monsoon, apparently wishing to escape from unduly damp localities. In many parts of Central and Southern India the bird resides permanently.

It is found in pairs for about half the year, from April to October, and at other times singly. It nests in India from June to October, laying from four to nine eggs in a hollow on the ground, usually unlined. These eggs are a little smaller than those of the common quail, and are much speckled with dark markings; the ground colour varies from yellowish white to rusty.

I may mention that the species has been recently bred in captivity in England by Mr. Seth-Smith, a Member of the Avicultural Society; this is interesting as showing that this bird, naturally confined to a warm climate, can nevertheless, like so many such species, bear and propagate in a colder one.

The note of the male Rain Quail is quite different from that of the common quail, consisting of two notes only, like "whit-whit."

The Blue-breasted or Painted Quail.

Excalfactoria chinensis, Faun. Brit. Ind., Birds., Vol. IV, p. 112.

NATIVE NAMES :—*Khair-butai*, *Kaneli*, Nepaulese ; *Gobal-butai*, Oudh ; *Ngon*, Burmese ; *Pandura-watuwa*, *Wenella-watuwa*, Cingalese.

This exquisite little creature is the smallest member of the pheasant family found with us, and both sexes are easily distinguished from our other quails by their very small size and bright yellow legs. Above, both cock and hen are much like the common quail, with a similar intricate mixture of buff, brown, and black ; below, they are very different, both from these and from each other. The cock has a slate-blue breast, the colour extending more or less on to the flanks, and a rich chestnut belly ; the throat is boldly marked with black and white somewhat as in the Rain Quail. The hen has a buff face, and is buff below with more or less well-defined black cross-bars. Cocks have red eyes, and hens and young cocks brown ones. The legs are, as above stated, bright yellow.

This bird is only about six inches long, with a wing of about half that length ; it only weighs about two ounces.

Small and fragile though it looks, however, this tiny quail has a wide range in South-Eastern Asia, from India to China and Siam. It also possesses a hardy constitution, for, unlike most birds of its family, it seeks rather than avoids wet ground. Thus it is unknown in the dry regions of North-

West India, and common in the moister districts of Bengal and Burma. Indeed, it migrates to some extent in search of damp situations, arriving in Lower Burma in May to be in time for the rains, though in Bengal it is commonest in the cold weather. Its haunts are in rank grass on wet land, and it is often found round paddy-fields. In India and Burma it breeds in June and July, but in Ceylon during the three months previous to these. At these times it is found in pairs, but at other times in coveys. The nest is in the usual hollow in the ground, grass-lined, and contains not more than half-a-dozen eggs, rather bigger than one would expect such a small bird to lay, being about an inch long. They are drab in colour, with more or less of a minute brown speckling. Not much else seems to be known about this little creature in the wild state, but its habits have been carefully studied of late years by certain good observers, members of the Avicultural Society, who have kept and bred it in confinement in England. It turns out to be a most interesting pet, hardly enough to bear our English winters in an outdoor aviary, and a free breeder if growing grass can be provided for it to nest in. The cock is a most attentive husband, calling his hen to take any tit-bit he may obtain, after the gallant fashion of the common fowl. He occasionally utters a tiny crow, resembling a miniature imitation of the "brain-fever-bird's" note. The hen is a prolific layer in captivity, and a good sitter and mother, and the chicks are easy to rear, and the most charming little creatures imaginable; they are literally not larger than the big black bees we are all so familiar with in India, and they can squeeze through half-inch mesh wire-netting! Although they take almost as long to hatch as common fowls, they mature with remarkable rapidity; Mr. Meade-Waldo, who was the first to breed them in England, found that his young cocks, when only just over a month old, had already assumed the proper plumage of their sex, and were actually crowing and calling their little sisters to feed! It is therefore very obvious that, though this minikin quail can hardly be regarded as game, it is pre-eminently suited for a pet; ordinary bird-seed keeps it well, with the addition of a few insects and crumbled hard-boiled egg for the young.

The quails that remain to be dealt with all agree in having distinct tail-feathers, though the tail is still short and inconspicuous in all except one species.

This one is the mountain-quail (*Ophrysia superciliosa*), in which the tail is three inches long; of the rest, the two typical bush-quails (*Perdicula*) are recognisable by their short, stout, almost bullfinch-like bills and their tail of twelve feathers, and the slight-billed bush-quails (*Microperdix*) by having a bill much like an ordinary quail's and ten feathers in the tail, which is more than half as long as the wing.

All the above birds are rather miniature partridges than quails, both in form and habits, the stout-billed bush-quails especially, in which the males have a little knob on each shank, representing a spur.

The Jungle Bush-Quail.

Perdicula asiatica, Faun. Brit. India, Birds, Vol. IV., p. 118.

NATIVE NAMES :—*Lowa*, Hind ; *Juhar*, in Manbhum ; *Auriconnai*, Sonthal ; *Girza pitta*, Telegu ; *Kari lowga*, Canarese.

The male of this species is brown above, mottled and pencilled with black and buff ; the head is mostly of a bright chestnut with white eyebrows, and the underparts conspicuously barred across with black and white. The female has the same chestnut head, but no barring below, the whole plumage being a nearly uniform light brown.

The young have no chestnut on the head, and a brown plumage streaked with buff above and whitish below.

In all the pinion-quills are plain brown on the inner web and spotted with buff on the outer.

The bill is black, the eyes brown, and the legs are orange.

This, although a thick-set little bird, is decidedly smaller than the common or grey quail, being only a little over six inches long, with a wing of a little over three inches and tail about half as long.

It inhabits well-wooded tracts in the Indian Peninsula, and also in the northern part of Ceylon. It is almost always in little flocks, from half-a-dozen to more than twice that number going about together, shooting off in all directions when alarmed, but quickly collecting again. Their call is a long trilling whistle, something like that which forms so large a part of the song of the German " Roller " canaries. They live on grass-seed and insects, and are themselves rather dry and not so good to eat as the true quails.

They breed from September to February, laying five to seven creamy-white eggs about an inch long in a nest of grass under the shelter of some bush or tussock. Although so sociable in a state of nature, they will fight in captivity, and are sometimes kept for this purpose by natives.

The Rock Bush-Quail.

Perdicula argunda, Faun. Brit. India, Birds, Vol. IV., p. 119.

NATIVE NAMES.—*Lowa*, Hind. and Mahratta; *Lawunka*, Telegu; *Sinkadeh*, Tamil; *Kemp lowga*, Kanarese of Mysore.

This species is very like the last. but is slightly larger, and differs in a few points in the plumage; there is more buff on the upper surface, the head is dull brick-red with no white eyebrow; the cock has broader bars below, and the hen a whitish chin and abdomen. But the chief difference is that the inner webs of the pinion-quills are spotted with buff as well as the outer.

This species, like the last, is a bird of the Indian Peninsula, but has a more restricted range, nor is it found in Ceylon. It also affects more open and drier county, chiefly inhabiting sandy or rocky ground with scanty vegetation; its nest and eggs are like those of its ally, as are its general habits; it breeds in August and September and also in March.

The slight-billed bush-quails, with longer tails and shorter wings than the above two species, and without spur-rudiments in the males, nevertheless closely resemble them in habits.

The Painted Bush-Quail.

Microperdix erythrorhynchus, Faun. Brit. Ind., Birds, Vol. IV., p. 121.

NATIVE NAME :—*Kodai*, Tamil.

The general colour of this bird is brown, warming into chestnut below, and distinctly spotted with black, the spots being especially large and bordered with white on the flanks and under the tail. The head of the cock is curiously marked with black and white, the chin, crown, and a patch round the eyes being black, while the throat and a band along each side of the head are white, the former having a black border ; the hen's face is dull reddish, with no black and white markings. The legs and bill are bright red, a point which at once distinguishes this species and the next from all our other quails. Young birds are like the hen, but have the black crown, which is nearly or quite absent in females.

The cock, which is a little larger than the hen, is seven inches long, with a wing of three-and-a-half inches and a two-inch tail.

This bird haunts the forests on and near the Western Ghauts, and is also common on the Nilgiris, while it has been obtained on the Shevaroys. Its call is different from that of the stout-billed bush quail, and it flies less noisily, being a softer-feathered bird. The breeding season varies, being from August to April according to local circumstances; the eggs are simply laid on the ground, are pale glossy cream-colour, and measure a little over an inch in length.

Blewitt's Bush-Quail.

Microperdix blewitti, Faun. Brit. Ind., Birds, Vol. IV, p. 122.

NATIVE NAME:—*Sirsi lawa*, in the Central Provinces.

This is hardly a distinct species, differing from the painted bush-quail only in being smaller and greyer, with a distinctly smaller bill and with more white and less black on the face of the male. It inhabits the forest region of the eastern Central Provinces.

Hume's Bush-Quail.

Microperdix manipurensis, Faun. Brit. Ind., Birds, Vol. IV, p. 122.

NATIVE NAME.—*Lanz-Soibol*, Manipuri.

One of Mr. Hume's most striking discoveries in Manipur, this pretty quail is very distinct in appearance from all our species. Its plumage is slate-colour, mottled with black above, and buff below the breast, this colour broken up into large spots by black markings which form a cross on every feather. The cock has a dark bay face, which at once distinguishes him from the hen. The bill is dark horny, and the legs orange.

In length this species is about seven inches, with a wing a little over three, and a tail of two inches.

Mr. Hume discovered this species himself when in Manipur, and obtained nine specimens (all he saw except two which were lost) after immense labour and two days' beating in an expanse of elephant grass covering broken ground about two miles square. The birds were in two coveys, and those shot were found to have fed upon both seeds and insects. A single bird was shot ten days later in the same district, and there is a specimen in the British Museum said to be from Sikkim. But except for these few specimens, nothing more was known of the Manipur bush-quail till 1899, nearly twenty years after Mr. Hume's discovery of the bird, when Captain H. S. Wood, of the Indian Medical Service, presented one to the Indian museum, and Lieutenant H. H. Turner two others. Captain Wood, who had found the species quite common in Manipur, afterwards wrote an interesting note on it in the Asiatic Society's *Journal* for 1899. He had shot about eighty of these quail, and did not consider them at all uncommon. The native name means "*Trap Quail*," as the Nagas snare numbers of them in nooses after jungle fires. The birds breed in Manipur, and the egg is large in proportion to the size of the bird, and greenish in colour with black and brown patches; unfortunately Captain Wood's specimens of them got broken in transit. He found the birds hard to see except after the jungle fires from February to April as they kept to dense cover, and even after a fire their dark colour made them hard to see on the burnt grass; they were always found close to water. The coveys kept very close when running, and Captain Wood has bagged as many as four at a shot.

The bird is thus pretty well known now, and what is chiefly wanted are birds in young plumage and a well-authenticated set of the eggs, which would appear from the description above given to differ from those of the common painted bush-quail as much as does the plumage of the parents.

Inglis' Bush-Quail.

Microperdix inglisi, Grant, Journ. Bom. Nat. Hist. Soc., Vol. XIX, p. 1.

NATIVE NAME:—*Kala goondri*, Goalpara district.

This is hardly more than a local race of the last species from which it differs chiefly in the reduction of the black markings, which form mere pencillings above on the grey back, and are narrower on the buff breast. It was discovered by Mr. C. M. Inglis in the Goalpara district, where it is plentiful, but Mr. Ogilvie Grant of the British Museum considers that a specimen said to have been procured in the Bhutan Dooars and received from the Calcutta Museum in 1893 belongs probably to this race.

The Mountain Quail.

Ophrysia superciliosa, Faun. Brit. Ind., Birds, Vol. IV, p. 105.

The Mountain quail—so called, for it is the least quail-like of all these little birds—is rather larger than the common grey quail, with a decidedly long tail for a bird of the kind, this appendage being fully as long as or longer than any ordinary partridge's, although all but covered above and below by the long tail-coverts. The general feathering is also of a long type, but the wings are decidedly short, and the colouring will at once distinguish the bird from any other of the family. The cock and hen, though neither is brilliantly coloured, are absolutely unlike each other, the former being slate-grey, tinged with olive above, and with black edgings to the sides of the feathers, a black head streaked with white, and black under-tail-coverts spotted with white; while the latter is brown, spotted with black centres to the feathers and the face a sort of pinkish grey.

Remnants of the young plumage on some specimens in the British Museum seem to show that both sexes when young have a garb of closely mottled black, brown and buff, so that they might easily be passed over as of no particular account if the comparatively large tail were not noticed.

The bill is red, bright coral in the male and dusky in the female, and the legs are dull red. In a pair kept in England the bill and legs were yellow. The length is about ten inches, with the tail three, the wing being only three and-a-half, and the shank one.

The mountain quail was described in 1846 by J. E. Gray from living specimens in the fine collection of the Earl of Derby at Knowsley Hall, and he gave the locality as "India" with a query. Nothing more was heard of it till 1865, when Kenneth Mackinnon shot a pair in November, in a hollow between Budraj and Benog, behind Mussoorie, at about 6,000 feet elevation. Again, in November, but two years later, at least one party established themselves at Jerepani, and remained till the summer of 1868; and five specimens were procured. Then, in December 1876, Major G. Carwithen got one bird on the eastern slopes of Sher-ka-danda, close to Naini Tal, at an elevation of 7,000 feet. No specimens have turned up since. It seems to be a migratory bird, arriving in winter, although its small wings look ill-adapted for a journey of any length. It goes in single pairs or coveys, and keeps close to cover in grass jungle or brushwood, being almost impossible to flush without a dog. Its flight is heavy, slow, and short; its food, grass seeds. The call is a shrill whistle. Anyone coming across these birds again should do his best to secure a living pair or two, and either breed from them himself—which could probably be done in the hills in a well-grassed run—or send them Home to the London Zoological Gardens or down to the Calcutta Gardens. In this way eggs might be obtained, whereas we are likely to wait a long time for them if we look to the discovery of a nest in the wild state in the case of such a rare and erratic bird as this one appears to be.

The true Grouse (*Tetraoninæ*) though none of them are found in Indian limits, are most important game-birds in Northern and Central Asia. They differ from Pheasants and Partridges chiefly in having the toes either feathered or, if naked, as is more often the case, fringed with narrow scales, so as to increase the bearing-surface of the foot. They never have spurs, their legs are always more or less feathered, and so is the covering of the nostrils; and in all Old-World species there is a red comb over the eye, greatly distended in the males in the breeding-season. The wings are rather longer than is usual in the Pheasant family, and Grouse fly better than most of these; but there is so little difference in general structure and habits that the separation of the Grouse as a distinct family from the Pheasants and Partridge is not justifiable, though usual in books. Several species of Grouse have hybridised with members of the Pheasant group, whereas hybrids between truly distinct families of birds are quite unknown.

Of the forest-grouse, which perch much, and have the legs feathered, but the toes bare and fringed with scales, Asia has the following species:—

Blackgame.

Lyrurus tetrix, Brit. Mus. Cat., Birds, Vol. XXII, p. 55.

NATIVE NAMES:—*Tetereff* for the cock and *Kosach* for the hen, in Russian.

The male, or Blackcock, is about as big as a Pheasant, glossy blue-black in colour except for a white bar on the wing and a white patch under the tail, the tail being strongly forked. The female or grey hen is smaller; with a shorter but still forked tail, and brown plumage barred across with black. This species ranges from Great Britain east at least as far as Manchuria; it is polygamous, and collects in the spring at certain play-places, showing off on the ground, the hen lays in May six to twelve pale buff eggs well speckled with chocolate.

Caucasian Blackgame.

Lyrurus mlokosiewiczi, Brit. Mus. Cat., Birds, Vol. XXII, p. 59.

NATIVE NAMES:—*Jaban tank*, Persian; *Paitmorek*, Armenian; *Kara-touch*, Tartar.

Confined to the Caucasus Mountains, this species is distinguished from the common blackgame by the cock being entirely black, with a much longer tail, and the hen having her brown plumage much more finely and closely marked—pencilled rather than barred; her tail is also longer than that of the common grey hen by about an inch. The eggs are paler than those of the last species.

Capercailzie.

Tetrao urogallus, Brit. Mus. Cat., Birds, Vol. XXII, p. 62.

NATIVE NAMES:—*Glouhar* for the cock and *Kopoluha* for the hen, in Russian.

This is the largest of the grouse, the cock being as big as a small hen turkey, with a large pale yellowish bill and medium length, rounded tail; the general plumage is iron-grey, brown and black, with a few white markings, the breast metallic dark-green. The hen, which is much smaller, is very like the grey hen, but has not the tail forked, and is much larger, two feet instead of a foot and-a-half long. The Capercailzie ranges all across Northern Europe and Asia as far as Lake Baikal; in the Southern Urals there is a very light-coloured race or sub-species, *Tetrao uralensis*. This species is polygamous, like the Blackcock, but shows off to the hens on a tree, not on the ground like that species; hybrids between them are not uncommon, and the cocks are easily known by their intermediate size, slightly-forked tails and metallic-purple breasts. The number of eggs and date of laying are the same as those of the grey hen, and the eggs are similar but bigger.

Black-billed Capercailzie.

Tetrao parvirostris, Brit. Mus. Cat., Birds, Vol. XXII, p. 66.

Occupying a range to the eastward of the common Capercailzie, from lake Baikal to Saghalien, this species is readily distinguishable from that bird by its smaller and black bill, blue-glossed head, and proportionally longer tail, which has no white markings. In the hen, which is very like the common Capercailzie hen, the tail is also longer, nearly eight inches as against barely seven-and-a-half. In Kamtschatka there is a race of this bird (*T. kamtschaticus*), which is distinguished by having continuous bands of white on the upper tail-coverts of the cock and the shoulders of the hen, where in the ordinary bird there are only rows of white spots.

The Black-billed Capercailzie 'plays' on the ground like the Blackcock, to which, as will be seen, it approaches in some points of appearance. Its eggs are longer than those of the common Capercailzie.

Spruce-Grouse.

Falcipennis falcipennis, Brit. Mus. Cat., Birds, Vol. XXII, p. 72.

NATIVE NAME:—*Karáka*, Tungus.

This grouse, distinguished by the narrow, curved form of the four outer wing-feathers, is of a mottled brown colour above, mottled black-and-white below; the tail, except the centre-feathers, is black with a white tip. The cock has a black throat and is darker generally than the hen. In size the Spruce-grouse is rather larger than the common partridge; it is a bird of North-East Siberia, ranging east to Kamtschatka and Saghalien.

Hazel-Grouse or Hazel-Hen.

Tetrastes bonasia, Brit. Mus. Cat., Birds, Vol. XXII, p. 89; *Yezo Kai-cho, Yamadori*, Japanese; *Riabchik*, Russian.

This little grouse, only the size of a partridge, has the legs only feathered half-way down; its plumage is mottled with a more or less greyish brown and black, and with much white below, and it has a distinctive mark in the tail, of which the feathers, except the centre ones, have a broad black band before the white tip, contrasting with the mottled grey of the rest of the feather. The cock is distinguished from the hen by his black throat. Ranging from Scandinavia across Europe and Asia to Japan, this widely-spread grouse especially frequents deciduous woods, unlike most of these forest-grouse which prefer conifers. About a dozen yellowish scantily spotted eggs are laid by it in May.

Mongolian Hazel-Grouse.

Tetrastes sevrtzovi, Brit. Mus. Cat., Birds, Vol. XXII, p. 93.

This species, which ranges from the Kansu Mountains to the Hoang-ho, affecting conifer forests, can be distinguished from the common hazel-hen by being barred with black all down the back, not only on the upper part, and by the outer tail-feathers being barred with white on a black ground.

The feather-toed grouse, or Ptarmigans (*Lagopus*) to which group the British Red Grouse belongs, are essentially birds of the wastes of the high north; all, except the Red Grouse, turn white in winter.

Willow Grouse.

Lagopus lagopus, Brit. Mus. Cat., Birds, Vol. XXII, p. 40. *Koropatka*, Russian.

In summer this bird is of a pencilled reddish-brown colour, richer in the cock than the hen, just like our Red Grouse in fact, but with the wings and belly white; in winter it is all white except the black outside tail-feathers. It ranges all round the world in the high north, and in Asia comes as far south as the Amoor. It frequents open bushy country, and packs in winter; the female lays about a dozen heavily-spotted eggs late in May.

Rock Ptarmigan.

Lagopus rupestris, Brit. Mus. Cat., Birds, Vol. XXII.

This is a more northern bird even than the willow-grouse, being found in the high Arctic regions all across Asia and America and in Iceland ; it is practically a race of the well-known Ptarmigan (L. *mutus*) of European mountain-tops. It is distinguished from the Willow-grouse at all seasons by its weaker bill and slightly smaller size, the closed wing of the cock being only seven and-a-half instead of eight inches; and in the white winter dress the cock has a black patch between bill and eye. In summer the coloured parts of his plumage are much blacker than those of the cock willow-grouse.

The eggs are very similar to those of the Willow-grouse, but smaller.

CHAPTER X.

Megapodes and Button-Quails.

The family of Megapodes or Mound-birds (*Megapodiidæ*) are always acknowledged to be near relatives of the *Phasianidæ*, differing chiefly in their long hind-toe and curious habit of burying their eggs, which disclose full-fledged young. Only one species is found in Indian limits.

The Nicobar Megapode or Mound-bird.

Megapodius nicobariensis, Faun. Brit. Ind., Birds, Vol. IV, p. 147.

In general appearance this bird resembles a large dull-brown partridge, with very short tail and huge legs and feet, of which the hind-toe is large and set on at the same level as the other toes, as in a pigeon. The claws of all the toes are long, broad, and nearly straight. The wings, although of blunt and rounded form, are larger than is usual in partridges. The plumage is plain dull brown, redder above and greyer below, becoming quite grey on the head; there is none of the marking or pencilling usual in partridges. The cock and hen are alike; young ones have no grey tinge below. The skin round the eyes is bare and red. The bill is yellowish or greenish and the legs horn-colour, becoming reddish at the back; the eyes are brown. The length is sixteen inches, the closed wing measuring nine and the tail three, while the shank is nearly three, and very strong.

This species is confined to the Nicobars, and is a very outlying member of its family, none being found nearer than the Philippines and Celebes, while most of them inhabit the Australian region. Its general habits are those of a jungle-fowl ; it is found in pairs or flocks, does not fly unless pressed, and readily perches. Unlike jungle-fowl, however, it appears to be a nocturnal bird. It has a cackling note, and feeds both on small animal life and vegetable food, being itself most delicious to eat, according to Mr. Hume, who compares it to a fat turkey and pheasant.

The huge eggs, which are more than three inches long, and pink when new-laid, are buried by the birds in a mound of vegetable matter and sand, which they scratch up in the jungle close to the shore. There their responsibility ceases ; the eggs hatch out by themselves in the mound, and the young come out of the egg fledged and able to fly, work their way to the upper air, and go off on their own account ; they look not unlike dull-brown quails.

In 1900 four of these birds were presented to the Calcutta Zoological Garden by Colonel Anson, and lived there for some time. These were hatched from eggs which had been taken from a mound in the Nicobars and brought up to the Andamans without any attention at all, so that this species is hardy enough in the egg. The young birds were reared on white ants, and were very tame when they came to Calcutta.

The species or races allied to this Megapode which are found in the islands belonging zoologically to Asia are all very like ours.

Cuming's Megapode.

Megapodius cumingi, Brit. Mus. Cat., Birds, Vol. XXII, p. 449.

This species inhabits the Philippines, Celebes, Palawan, Tojian, the Sulu islands, and the little islands off the North Bornean coast. It is darker than the Nicobar bird, especially where the plumage is grey.

Sanghir Megapode.

Megapodius sanghirensis, Brit. Mus. Cat., Birds, Vol, XXII, p. 450.

Confined to the Sanghir islands, this Megapode is characterised by being dark brown below instead of grey; it is darker than the Nicobar bird.

Bernstein's Megapode.

Megapodius bernsteini, Brit. Mus. Cat., Birds, Vol. XXII, p. 450.

This characteristic race of the Sulu islands of the Celebes group is also brown below, but the brown is of a reddish shade, and the tail is dull black. . It is smaller than the species above-mentioned, the closed wing measuring less than eight inches.

In North Celebes and the Sanghir islands is found a very curious and distinct member of the Megapode family, with no near relations.

Malbo.

Megacephalon maleo, Brit. Mus. Cat., Birds, Vol. XXII, p. 472.

This bird is about the size of a jungle-fowl, and the tail is much like that of a jungle-hen; the feet are of ordinary size, and the head naked, with a large rounded helmet at the back, black in colour; the plumage also is nearly black, being a very dark brown, except the under-parts, which are salmon-pink. The sexes are alike, but the young have a feathered head and no helmet. This handsome bird does not throw up a mound to bury its eggs in, but buries them in holes in the black sand of volcanic beaches, coming for some distance from the forests—where it usually lives—to do this, in the months of August and September; the eggs are over four inches long and of a pale reddish hue.

Button-Quails.—(*Turnicidæ*).

I have already, in the beginning of the last chapter, drawn attention to the fact that the Button-Quails or Hemipodes do not belong to the *Phasianidæ* at all, not being true quails, and have pointed out their external differences from the latter. To briefly summarise the most striking of these differences again, I may mention that the Indian Button-Quails have no hind toe, and have, in life, distinctly yellowish-white eyes, which give them a very different expression. In general habits they resemble the true quails, but the males are always smaller than the females, and are altogether the inferior sex, sitting on the eggs and taking care of the young, while the hens are bold and pugnacious, fighting like the males of the true quails, and not at all domestically inclined. The Button-Quails can hardly be seriously regarded as objects of spot, but they are good to eat.

The Blue-legged Button-Quail.

Turnix pugnax, Faun. Brit. Ind., Birds, Vol. IV, p. 151.

NATIVE NAMES:—*Gulu*, *Gundlu*, *Salui-gundru*, Hindi; *Koladu* (male), *Pured* (female). Telugu; *Aukádeh* (male), *Kurungkadeh* (female), Tamil; *Durwa*, Ratnagiri; *Káre-haki*, Kanarese in Mysore; *Timok*, Lepcha; *Ngon*, Burmese.

This bird is often called the "Bustard-quail" in books, but the name is distinctly misleading, as this species is as unlike a bustard as are the rest.

The general colouring of the male of this species above is a complicated mixture of brown, black, and white, more reddish in some specimens than in others; below it is buff, with a whitish throat and black bars across the breast. In the female the throat is black, and the middle of the breast black also to a greater or less extent. Young birds have black spots on the breast instead of bars.

The bill and legs in this species are blue-grey, and, with the barred breast, conspicuously distinguish it.

The cock is six inches long, with a wing of about three inches; the hen about half an inch longer, with a noticeably stronger bill. In captivity I have seen her eat whole butterflies two inches across the wings.

This bird is found all over the Empire except in the higher parts of the hills and in Sind and the Punjab; it avoids deserts and heavy forest; out of India it ranges east to China and Formosa. It usually breeds in the rainy season, sometimes simply laying in a hollow, and sometimes making a domed nest. The eggs are usually four, greyish with reddish and brown markings, and nearly an inch long. The variation of colour in this bird follows the climate it inhabits, the darkest and greyest specimens coming from districts where there is a heavy rainfall; these individuals evidently having a constitution more suited for resisting damp. It is, of course, possible that a damp climate may have a direct effect on the plumage, but this could only be established by keeping the reddish specimens from a dry tract in an open-air aviary in a damp district, and observing if they moulted out greyer.

The Yellow-legged Button-Quail.

Turnix tanki, Faun. Brit. Ind., Birds, Vol. IV, p. 153.

NATIVE NAMES :—*Lowa*, *Lowa-butai*, Hindi ; *Pedda daba gundlu*, Telegu.

This is about the same size as the last species, but is less speckled above and more inclined to a plain drab; moreover, at certain seasons, the hens have a chestnut half-collar at the back of the neck. The underparts are buff without bars, but with black spots at the sides of the breast. Young birds are redder and more speckled above. The bill and legs are bright yellow, with a black streak along the ridge of the bill in males.

The bird is found all over India, including Sind, but does not usually range above 4,000 feet in the hills. In April 1898, however, Mr. Goldstein, the Chemist at the Chowrasta in Darjeeling, showed me a live specimen he had captured there under very peculiar circumstances : it was flying round and round a lamp where he used to catch moths, and he caught it in a butterfly-net

Its breeding time is in July and August in Upper India, but in Mysore about April, and its eggs are of a similar type to those of the last species. Mr. D. Seth-Smith has bred it in England, and finds the incubation-period to be only twelve days, whereas the equally small Painted Quail takes three weeks. The hen Button-quail is so masculine in her character that during courtship she gives her mate any tit-bit she may obtain, just as the common cock and some others of the true game-birds do with their females! Moreover, she does not care at all for her young, but eats the food they ought to have.

The Burmese Yellow-legged Button-Quail.

Turnix blanfordi, Faun. Brit. Ind., Birds, Vol. IV, p. 156.

NATIVE NAME :—*Ngon*, Burmese

This is hardly a distinct species, but merely a large local race of the last one, the females being seven inches long as against the six and-a-half inches of the Indian specimens. The plumage, however, is distinguishable in adult specimens by the greater amount of black barring on the back. This species ranges from Assam and Chittagong to China; of course extending through Burma

The Nicobar Yellow-legged Button-Quail.

Turnix albiventris, BLANFORD, Faun. Brit. Ind., Birds, Vol. IV, p. 154.

This is another local race of *Turnix tanki*, not exceeding it in size, but more mottled with black and reddish on the back in adults, and with the female's collar of a darker chestnut. It is confined to the Andamans and Nicobars, and rare in the former group of islands. "Species" like this and the last are really better distinguished by the American system of "trinomials" so as to stand as *Turnix tanki blanfordi*, and *T. tanki albiventris*. While it would hardly do to ignore them, I think it is rather absurd to give them full specific rank

The White-legged or Little Button-Quail.

Turnix dussumieri, Faun. Brit. Ind., Birds, Vol. IV, p. 152.

NATIVE NAMES:—*Ghinwa lowa*, *Chota lawa*, *Dabki*, *Tura*, *Chimnaj* (in Muttra); *Libbia* (in Purneah), Hindi; *Darwi*, Ratnagiri; *Chinna* or *Tella dabba gundlu*, Telegu; *San gundlu*, Uriya.

This species is at once distinguished from the others by its smaller size and lighter colour, besides its funny little pointed tail, which is long enough to be noticeable, while those of our other Button-quails are not so any more than are those of the typical quails. Above it is mostly chestnut mixed with cream-colour, and nearly white below, running into buff on the breast, with black spots on the sides of the latter. Male and female are alike in colour, and the former is in this species not very much the smaller. The bill is blue-grey and the feet fleshy white. At times I have seen birds of this species in the Calcutta market with blue-grey legs, but in the case of such specimens the characteristic points given above will afford a means of distinction from the blue-legged Button-quail. The hen is five-and-a-half inches long, with a wing of nearly three inches.

This bird inhabits most of India and Burma, but not Ceylon, nor does it seem to occur south of Mysore, nor does it range high up the hills. It extends eastward to Hainan and Formosa. Its breeding season is from April to October, and the eggs, laid in a hollow lined with grass, may sometimes be as many as six. They are stone-coloured with a fine brownish speckling and larger spots of darker brown, and measure about four-fifths of an inch in length.

Philippine Button-Quail.

Turnix fasciata, Brit. Mus. Cat., Birds, Vol. XXII, p. 535.

This is very like the Blue-legged Button-quail (*T. pugnax*) of India, but has yellow legs and bill, and females are darker, with a very clear chestnut collar. It is found in the Philippines and Palawan.

Celebean Button-Quail.

Turnix rufilatus, Brit. Mus. Cat., Birds, Vol. XXII, p. 536.

This Celebean species also combines yellow legs and bill with a plumage generally similar to that of the Indian Blue-legged species, but the cock has the light barring on the chest white, not buff, and the hen has the throat barred black and white, not all black.

Whitehead's Button-Quail.

Turnix whiteheadi, GRANT, Game-Birds, Vol. II, p. 276.

Only a few specimens of this little species, which is much like the little white-legged Indian bird, have been obtained, near Manilla ; it is distinguished from the above Indian species by having the prevailing colour of the upper parts blackish-grey, not chestnut and buff.

Chestnut-Breasted Button-Quail.

Turnix ocellata, Brit. Mus. Cat., Birds, Vol. XXII, p. 548.

This bird, confined to Luzon, is about the size of the larger Indian Button-Quails, and has yellow legs and bill ; it is drab, mottled with black above, and has a plain chestnut breast and buff abdomen ; the throat is white in the male, more or less black in the hen.

Sulu Button-Quail.

Turnix suluensis, MEARNS, Proc. Zool. Soc., Washington, Vol. XVIII, p. 83.

A female, the type of this species, obtained on Sulu in the Philippines, most resembled Whitehead's Button-quail, but was larger, brown in general tint above instead of blackish.

CHAPTER XI.

Sand-grouse.

The Sand-grouse (*Pteroclidæ*) have no relationship to the true grouse, but form a separate family of their own, very distinct from any other birds ; they come nearer to the pigeons and plovers than to the game-birds proper. They may be distinguished from any of these by having feathered legs with smooth-edged toes, the feather-legged true grouse having, as has been said above, fringes of scales along the sides of their toes. Two Sand-grouse have the toes as well as the legs feathered, like Ptarmigans, but they may be distinguished from these by having only three toes, the hind-toe being missing. The Sand-grouse, however, are so unlike any other old-world birds that they are not easily mistaken. They have a small bill and head like those of the true game-birds, but long-pointed wings like pigeons or some plovers ; their feet are small, and the hind-toe when present is always very small, and of no use. Their plumage is close, like that of pigeons, and shows a general sandy hue in most cases ; the sexes are always more or less different. Sand-grouse frequent dry, generally open, country in Europe, Africa and Asia ; they are often migratory. Most of the few species are found in Indian limits, where they are often called Rock-pigeons by sportsmen. Their flight is high and fast ; and their note usually a double or treble cluck.

They feed chiefly on seeds and herbage, go to water twice a day, and lay their three spotted eggs, which are elliptical, long and equally rounded at both ends, on the ground without a nest; both cock and hen sit on them. The spotting of the eggs is in two shades, as in many plovers, whereas those of the true game-birds only have one set of spots. The young are active at once, like game-chicks, but their down is of a different character, being in tiny tufts, not uniformly fluffy, and it is marbled in pattern instead of streaked. In two cases at least the parents bring the chicks water by soaking their breast feathers in it and then letting the young suck it off—a habit unique among birds. Sand-grouse are, generally speaking, of much about the same size —that of a common dove, though two or three are as large as pigeons. Beyond specifying these, therefore, I have not thought it worth while to give dimensions.

The Sand-grouse occurring in the Indian empire do not range east of the Bay of Bengal, they are divided into three genera :—

The *ordinary Sand-grouse* (*Pterocles*) with short-pointed tails (6 species).

The *Pin-tailed Sand-grouse* (*Pteroclurus*) which only differ in having the two centre tail-feathers long and pointed (3 species).

The Three-toed Sand-grouse (*Syrrhaptes*), which are much more distinct, having only three toes, very broad, short and feathered like the legs. (One species). It is as well to begin with the Pin-tailed group, as one of these is the commonest and best known of the family in India.

Common Pin-tailed Sand-Grouse.

Pteroclurus exustus, Faun. Brit. Ind., Birds, Vol. IV, p. 60.

NATIVE NAMES.—*Bhat-titar*, *Bakht-titar*, *Kumar-tit*, *Kahar*, Hind.; *Butabur*, *Batibun*, in Sind; *Popandi* of the Bhils; *Pakorade*, Maharatta; *Jam polanka*, Telegu; *Kal-gowjalhaki*, Canarese.

The general colour of the male of this bird is sandy, mixed with grey above, and with narrow chocolate tips on the small wing-feathers. The breast is crossed by a narrow black band, and below this the buff shades into the chocolate of the belly; the face and throat are pale yellow. The hen is buff, barred with black, the black marks, however, forming streaks on the head and breast; the abdomen is dark brown, barred with buff. The long "pin-feathers" in the tail are shorter than in the cock. The bill and feet are grey and the eyelids pale yellow: the eyes dark, as in all our Sand-grouse.

In dry open districts of the plains this Sand-grouse may be looked for everywhere in India except generally in Bengal (though one once occurred even in the Calcutta Botanic Gardens) and the Coast of Bombay and Malabar. Its range extends westward to Senegal. In India it is resident, and may be found nesting at any time, though most generally in the earlier half of the year. The eggs are greyish, pinkish, or buff, with the usual grey or brown markings. Like other Sand-grouse, they are very regular in their ways, drinking at from 8 to 10 in the morning and again from 4 to 6 in the afternoon, and resting in the middle of the day. Their note is a double cluck, and, as with sand-grouse generally, is usually uttered on the wing.

Spotted Pin-tailed Sand-Grouse.

Pteroclurus senegallus, Faun. Brit. Ind., Birds, Vol. IV, p. 61.

NATIVE NAMES.—*Nundu Katinga, Gutu*, in Sind.

The general colour of the cock of this species is also sandy, with a buff throat, but his wings are indistinctly mottled with chocolate, and there is a grey band along each side of the head. The belly is dark brown, but there is no black breast-band. The hen is buff, very distinctly *spotted* with black, not barred or mottled, as in our other hen Sand-grouse. This species is rare with us except in Sind, west of the Indus, though it extends to the Punjab. Westwards it ranges to Africa, even south of the Sahara, and most of those found in Sind are only winter visitors, though hens have been shot containing fully-formed eggs; the eggs are buff spotted with pale, brown and grey. The note of this species is different from that of other Sand-grouse, being a sort of gurgling sound like that produced by blowing through water.

Large Pin-Tailed Sand-Grouse.

Pteroclurus alchata, Faun. Brit. Ind., Birds, Vol. IV, p. 58.

This is a large species, equalling a pigeon in size and of remarkable beauty of plumage. The cock is of a peculiar sandy olive-green above, scantily mottled with yellow; a patch on the wing is beautifully coloured chocolate with narrow white edgings to the feathers, and the lower back is barred with black and buff; the throat is black, the breast buff, with two black bands set far apart, and the belly white. · This white belly and the buff breast bounded below by a black band, are also found in the hen, but she has two black bands on the upper breast, the higher much the broadest, and her upper parts are buff, barred with black. She has a variegated wing-patch like the cock, but this is black with broad white edgings. The feet are dirty green, and the bill greenish or grey.

This is a western bird, only visiting the north-west of India as a winter migrant; it is, however, very abundant at that season, associating in bigger packs than other Sand-grouse. It ranges westwards into Northern Africa and Southern Europe, and these most western specimens are more richly coloured than ours. Its loud triple note can be heard for a long distance, and it is a very noisy bird.

Black-Bellied Sand-Grouse.

Pterocles arenarius, Faun. Brit. Ind., Birds, Vol. IV, p. 54.

NATIVE NAMES.—*Bhat titar*, *Bakht*, *Bakht-titar*, Hind.; *Banchurat*, Peshawar; *Burra Bhutta* in Hurriana; *Katinga*, in Sind.

Equalling a good large pigeon in size, this fine sand-grouse is also distinguished by very striking colouring; the cock is mottled with slate and yellow on the back, has a chestnut throat and neck, mark-

Copyright. L. Medland.

BLACK-BELLIED SAND-GROUSE, COCK.

Copyright. L. Medland.

BLACK-BELLIED SAND-GROUSE, HEN.

ed with a black patch, and contrasting with the grey head and breast; the breast is bordered below by a narrow black band, below which is a broad belt of cream-colour, the rest of the under-parts being black. The same black under-parts preceded by a cream belt are found in the hen, but her general plumage is very different, being buff, mottled with black. The bill and feet are grey, and the eyelids yellow.

The Black-bellied Sand-grouse is only a winter bird in India, and especially affects the extreme north-west, associating in enormous numbers on large sandy plains. Outside India it ranges west through Asia, North Africa, and Southern Europe, to the Canary Islands. It only breeds west of India as far as is known, though eggs have been taken as near as Southern Afghanistan in May; they are dull light buff, marked with light brown and dull lilac.

Coronetted Sand-Grouse.

Pterocles coronatus, Faun. Brit. Ind., Birds, Vol. IV, p. 57.

This species, only found with us in Sind west of the Indus, is very like the spotted Pin-tailed Sand-grouse in general appearance, but has not the long centre tail-feathers; the cock also has black marks on face and throat, and the hen is barred rather than spotted. Outside India this bird extends west to North-East Africa: eggs have been taken to Afghanistan, and are greyish white, scantily spotted with pale brown.

Painted Sand-Grouse.

Pterocles fasciatus, Faun. Brit. Ind., Birds, Vol. IV, p. 55.

NATIVE NAMES.—*Pahari bhat titar*, Hind. in the North-West Provinces; *Palki* in Belgaum; *Handeri* in Southern India; *Kalgowjalhaki*, Canarese of Mysore; *Sondapolanka*, Tamil.

This and the next differ from our other Sand-grouse in being less gregarious, frequenting less open country, and being rather nocturnal, coming to water before dawn and after dark. They would really have more right to be put in a separate genus than the Pin-tailed kinds. This small species is very distinctly and beautifully marked in the case of the male, which is broadly barred above with chocolate, slate and buff; the head is peculiarly marked, the forehead being white, followed by a large black patch, then by white again, while the rest is buff, streaked with black. The neck and breast are plain buff, bordered by a chocolate band; this is followed by a broad cream-coloured belt, bordered below by black; the belly is barred black and buff.

The hen is buff, finely barred with black both above and below, the barring extending even to the leg-feathering. The bill is reddish, the eyelids yellow and the feet dull yellow. Eyes dark as in all sand-grouse.

The painted sand-grouse is only found in India, and generally frequents rocky ground and low jungle, but in many districts it does not occur—it is not found west of the Indies nor in the Ganges delta, the Carnatic plains, the Bombay and Malabar coasts, or the forests north of the Godavery. It lays in April and May as a rule, and the eggs are salmon-pink in ground-colour.

Close-barred Sand-Grouse.

Pterocles lichtensteini, Faun. Brit. Ind., Birds, Vol. IV, p. 57.

The Close-barred Sand-grouse has a general similarity to its Painted ally, but the cock is much less handsome, being more narrowly barred, with black on a buff ground ; the upper breast is barred as well as the back. The hen is like that of the last species but more finely barred, and without any bars on the leg-feathering. In this species also there are only 14 tail-feathers, the Painted Sand-grouse having 16.

This species only lives, with us, in Sind, west of the Indus, which it is said to visit only in winter. It also inhabits Baluchistan, Arabia and the adjacent parts of Africa.

Of the three-toed Sand-grouse, only one species is found in Indian limits.

Tibetan Three-toed Sand-Grouse.

Syrrhaptes tibetanus, Faun. Brit. Ind., Birds, Vol. IV, p. 62.

NATIVE NAMES.—*Kuk*, *Kaling*, in Ladak.

The largest of all Sand-grouse, this bird is easily recognised by its three-toed feet, and by the short broad toes being covered, like the very short shanks, with feathers; the tail has long centre-feathers as in the Pin-tailed kinds. The general colour is sandy, finely pencilled with black; the throat is dull yellow, the quills black, and the belly white. The hen differs less from the cock than in other Sand-grouse, but has the black pencilling coarser, and extending all over the breast, the lower part of the cock's being plain. As its name implies, this is a bird of high Asia—Tibet and the Pamir, and Koko-nor, but it is also found in Ladak and the upper Sutlej valley. Its note, frequently uttered on the wing, sounds something like *Yuck-yuck*. It drinks very early in the morning and late in the evening. Eggs obtained on the Pamir are of the typical Sand-grouse shape, about two inches long, and cream-colour, sprinkled over with small brown and grey spots. The only other Asiatic Sand-grouse is also the only other near ally of this bird.

Pallas' Three-Toed Sand-Grouse.

Syrrhaptes paradoxus, Brit. Mus. Cat., Birds, Vol. XXII, p. 2.

NATIVE NAMES.—*Stepnaya kuritza*, Russian; *Sha-chee*, Chinese.

With the same peculiar feet and pin-tail, this is a much smaller species than the last, being of the turtle-dove size usual in sand-grouse. The cock is buff above, coarsely barred with black on the back. The throat is golden buff, the breast grey, ending in a band of black pencilling; then there is a broad cream-coloured belt, followed by a black patch; the hen is more finely pencilled with black above, has a narrow black line bordering the throat, and the breast spotted with black and without the bordering band, but with the cream belly and black belly patch as in the cock.

This species, which has on several occasions created an ornithological sensation by invading Western Europe, including Britain, inhabits the steppe-region from South Russia to North China. It has a triple note, like *truckturuck.* The eggs, laid about the beginning of June, are stone colour, marked with chocolate and purplish.

APPENDIX I.

SYNOPTICAL TABLE OF FULL-PLUMAGED MALES.

It is generally agreed among sportsmen that only full-plumaged males should be shot among game-birds, at any rate the polygamous species: and even among the pairing kinds there is apt to be a preponderance of cocks, while, as young cocks are generally like hens, if hen-coloured birds are spared, some cocks are sure to be left. Hence, as the common points of cock and hen, where these differ, are often difficult to give concisely, I give only a table of full-plumaged male game-birds.

Shanks bare throughout or nearly so; front toes webbed at base; hind toe small; wings short and rounded.	PHEASANT AND PARTRIDGE FAMILY.
A. Big birds, much larger than fowls, with tail or train four feet long.	
A. 1. Neck blue, a fan-shaped crest.	*Common Peacock* (p. 10).
A. 2. Neck green, a lance-head-shaped crest.	*Burmese Peacock* (p. 13).
A. 3. General plumage brown, wings extremely large.	*Argus Pheasant* (p. 40).
B. Birds about two feet long, with tails not longer than wing.	
B. 1. Breast red, spotted with white.	*Crimson Tragopan* (p. 28).
B. 2. Breast black, spotted with white.	*Black Tragopan* (p. 29).
B. 3. Breast red above, grey below, unspotted.	*Grey-breasted Tragopan* (p. 30).
B. 4. Breast velvety black ..	*Common Monaul* (p. 32).
B. 5. Breast glossy green ..	*Bronze-backed Monaul* (p. 35).

B. 6. Breast black-and-white above, grey below.	*Himalayan Snowcock* (p. 87).
B. 7. Breast grey above, black and white below.	*Tibetan Snowcock* (p. 88).
C. Birds of the size of fowls or smaller, with long tails.	
C. 1. A comb present; breast black.	*Red Jungle-fowl* (p. 15).
C. 2. A comb present; breast orange-red.	*Ceylon Jungle-fowl* (p. 19).
C. 3. A comb present; breast streaky grey.	*Grey Jungle-fowl* (p. 21).
C. 4. Tail flat and broad, with green eye-spots.	*Peacock-pheasant* (p. 45).
C. 5. Tail very long and arched; a ruff present.	*Lady Amherst's Pheasant* (p. 49).
C. 6. Tail long and pointed; a long crest.	*Cheer Pheasant* (p. 51).
C. 7. Tail long and pointed; no crest; wings and back marked with white.	*Mrs. Hume's Pheasant* (p. 54).
C. 8. Tail long and pointed; no crest; no white.	*Stone's Pheasant* (p. 57).
D. Size of small fowl; tail short and rounded; plumage grey, green and crimson.	*Blood-Pheasant* (p. 37).
E. Size of small fowl; tail short and pointed; three crests.	
E. 1. Front of neck chestnut. ..	*Common Koklass* (p. 63).
E. 2. Neck chestnut all round ..	*Chestnut Koklass* (p. 65).
F. About size of fowl; a long crest; face red; tail moderate and broad.	
F. 1. Blue-black above, whitish below; crest white.	*White-crested Kaleege* (p. 68).
F. 2. Blue-black above, whitish below; crest black, white bars on back.	*Nepaul Kaleege* (p. 69).
F. 3. Blue-black above, whitish below, crest black, no white on back.	*Black-backed Kaleege* (p. 70).
F. 4. Blue-black all over except white bars on back.	*Purple Kaleege* (p. 71).

F. 5. Grizzly grey above, black below.	*Lineated Kaleege* (p. 72).
I do not give any key to the more doubtful species of	Kaleege (p. 62).
G. Size of large fowl; face blue, tail moderate, broad.	*Fire-backed Pheasant* (p. 80).
H. Partridges with tails, more than half length of wing.	
H. 1. Shanks feathered half-way down, plumage barred; bill and feet red.	*Snow-partridge* (p. 91).
H. 2. Plumage mottled; bill and legs dull green.	*Tibetan Partridge* (p. 92).
H. 3. Plumage plain drab or grey above; bill and feet red.	*Chukor* (p. 93).
H. 4. Plumage barred throughout, throat buff, black-bordered.	*Grey Partridge* (p. 102).
H. 5. Plumage barred above, streaked below, throat chestnut.	*Swamp Partridge* (p. 104).
H. 6. Plumage mostly black including throat, spotted with white below.	*Black Partridge* (p. 106).
H. 7. Face chestnut, under-parts nearly covered with white spots.	*Painted Francolin* (p. 108).
H. 8. Plumage mostly black, spotted with white below, throat white.	*Chinese Francolin* (p. 109).
I. Spurfowl, partridge-like, with hen-like tails, aud double-spurred.	
I. 1. General colour chestnut ..	*Red Spurfowl* (p. 99).
I. 2. Chestnut spotted with white above, breast buff, black-spotted.	*Painted Spurfowl* (p. 100).
I. 3. Streaked black and white above, breast pure white.	*Ceylon Spurfowl* (p. 101).
J. Partridge with tail nearly as long as wing, belly buff with large black spots.	*Bamboo Partridge* (p. 112).
K. Partridges with very short tails, not noticeable; nails very long.	
K. 1. Throat black, bordered with white, breast grey.	*Common Hill-Partridge* (p. 114).

K. 2.	Throat chestnut, black-spotted; breast grey.	*Blyth's Hill-Partridge* (p. 115).
K. 3.	Throat black, not bordered with white; breast grey.	*Arakan Hill-Partridge* (p. 116).
K. 4.	Throat black, merging into grey breast, no chestnut on sides.	*White-cheeked Hill-Partridge* (p. 117).
K. 5.	Throat pale chestnut, chest darker, black and white band between.	*Red-breasted Hill-Partridge* (p. 118).
K. 6.	Throat buff, black-speckled, breast brownish buff.	*Brown-breasted Hill-Partridge* (p. 118).
K. 7.	Throat white, black-speckled, then chestnut, black-spotted, legs green.	*Green-legged Hill-Partridge* (p. 122).
L.	Partridge of dark glossy greenish-blue, with red crest. (Hen green, not crested, may easily be taken for different species.)	*Red-crested Partridge* (p. 124).
M.	Partridge with plumage mostly chestnut, back barred.	*Chestnut Wood-Partridge* (p. 123).
N.	Partridge with plumage sandy, bill and legs yellow.	*Seesee* (p. 96).
O.	Quails, very small, with closed wing under five inches, tail very short.	
O. 1.	Throat white, marked with dark brown, breast buff.	*Common Quail* (p. 129).
O. 2.	Throat white, marked with black, breast streaked with black.	*Rain Quail* (p. 135).
O. 3.	Throat brick-red, unmarked, breast buff.	*Japanese Quail* (p. 133).
O. 4.	Breast slaty-blue, belly rich chestnut; very small size.	*Painted Quail* (p. 137).
O. 5.	Throat chestnut, breast barred black and white, quills, plain on inner web, spotted buff on outer.	*Jungle Bush-Quail* (p. 140).

O. 6. Throat chestnut, breast barred black and white, quills spotted with buff on both webs.	*Rock Bush-Quail* (p. 141).
O. 7. Head black-and-white, sides with black white-edged spots.	*Painted Bush-Quail* (p. 142).
O. 8. As above, but plumage greyer and less black on face.	*Blewitt's Bush-Quail* (p. 143).
O. 9. Slate mottled with black above, mottled black and buff below.	*Hume's Bush-Quail* (p. 143).
O. 10. As above, but only pencilled with black above, less buff below.	*Inglis's Bush-Quail* (p. 145).
P. Quail with well-developed tail three inches long; plumage grey with black streaks.	*Mountain Quail* (p. 145).
Like large plain-brown partridge, but with large well-developed hind-toe, all nails very long.	NICOBAR MEGAPODE (p. 152).
Quail-like birds with three toes only ..	BUTTON-QUAILS.
1. Breast barred with black, legs blue-grey.	*Blue-legged Button-Quail* (p. 156).
2. Breast buff, black-spotted at sides, legs yellow.	*Yellow-legged Button-Quail* (p. 157).
3. As above, but more black on back.	*Burmese Yellow-legged Button-Quail* (p. 158).
4. As 2, but with more black and reddish on back.	*Nicobar Yellow-legged Button-Quail* (p. 159).
5. Very small, breast buff, black-spotted on sides, tail noticeably pointed, legs white or bluish-grey.	*Little Button-Quail* (p. 159).
Shanks short, feathered throughout, hind toe very small or wanting, wings long.	*Sand-grouse* (p. 162).
A. Toes naked, hind-toe present, centretail-feathers long and pointed.	
A. 1. Sandy above, belly chocolate, black breast-band.	*Common Pin-tailed Sand-grouse* (p. 164).

A. 2. Sandy above, grey band along sides of head, no black breast-band.	*Spotted Pin-tailed Sand-grouse* (p. 165).
A. 3. Olive-green above, yellow spotted, breast buff, belly white.	*Large Pin-tailed Sand-grouse* (p. 165).
B. Toes naked, hind-toe present, centre tail-feathers not projecting.	
B. 1. Mottled slate and yellow above, belly black.	*Black-bellied Sand-grouse* (p. 166).
B. 2. Sandy above, black marks on face and throat.	*Coronetted Sand-grouse* (p. 167).
B. 3. Broadly barred above with chocolate and buff.	*Painted Sand-grouse* (p. 168).
B. 4. Finely barred above with black and buff.	*Close-barred Sand-grouse* (p. 169).
C. No hind-toe; toes feathered like shanks; centre tail-feathers long.	*Tibetan Sand-grouse* (p. 169).

APPENDIX II.

Game Birds in Captivity.

As game-birds will generally live well in captivity, their management is well known, but a few hints to beginners may not be out of place; even if there is no idea of keeping these birds for any length of time, it may often be necessary to collect and transport them for re-stocking depleted areas, or for export abroad, and mistakes may easily be made by inexperienced people even in simple proceedings like these.

For instance, care is required in handling such birds; the larger ones are very strong and violent in their movements, and so are apt to hurt themselves when handled; while the smaller kinds have a way of slipping backwards out of one's grasp in a most disconcerting manner. In handling a quail or partridge, therefore, it is as well to be prepared for this manœuvre; a bigger bird should be grasped by the legs or wings, always taking hold of both at once, and seizing the legs high up. This last precaution is particularly necessary in the case of spurred species, whose weapons may inflict a nasty cut. A hand net is best to shift these birds with, whenever it can be used, as when catching them out of an aviary or enclosure.

Then, game-birds of all sorts are particularly apt to spring up violently and hurt their heads; hence, any basket, cage or hutch used for transporting them in should have a loose canvas or sacking top, this being protected above by a more solid roof if necessary. When confined in rooms or in aviaries, these should have a ceiling of fine string net some inches below the real roof, unless the birds are intended to be kept shut up permanently, when it will be sufficient to clip one of the wings of each specimen when they are put in; this will prevent any suicidal performances for some time, and by the time the cut quills are all moulted out the birds will have got tamer.

All aviaries for birds of this description should be roofed and kept as dry underfoot as possible; and shade is also very important in a climate like India; but an outdoor run attached is a very useful adjunct, and tends to keep the birds in better condition.

A third point to bear in mind in the treatment of captive game-birds is their fierce tempers; the sexes should never be kept mixed during or just before the breeding season, or there will be murder and mutilation among the cocks, though cocks alone can generally be kept together. When on a long journey, such as a voyage to Europe, it is just as well to keep each bird in a separate compartment, in the case of the larger species.

Feeding is a simple matter in the management of game-birds, a mixture of various sorts of corn and seeds suiting all of them; the little ones, of course, needing the smallest kinds only. In aviaries, this may be thrown among the litter on the floor, it being understood that this litter is frequently renewed—once a week or so; it should consist of chaff, or any such convenient substance, with some fine gravel to aid digestion, and some earth or sand for the birds to roll in, which they will do instead of bathing.

A small water vessel is all that is necessary except in the hot weather, when I have observed that pea-fowl, at any rate, like to stand in water. Care should be taken that the water is kept clean and cool.

Grain alone is not sufficient food if the birds are to be kept shut up for more than a week or so; in more prolonged captivity they should be given daily rations of raw vegetable food such as various salad vegetables, and these should be hung up in bunches so that they can be picked at and not dragged about. A frequent allowance of white-ants, or in default of such insects, some chopped cooked meat, is also desirable; chopped raw roots, such as potatoes and onions, and fruit, are very beneficial, especially to such species as Monauls, and should be among the rations provided for a sea-voyage.

All food, by the way, given during such a journey should be given in vessels securely fixed up, and none thrown on the floor, which should be a barred wooden grating an inch or two above the real bottom of the cage, so that all dirt will fall through and can be scraped out without disturbing the birds. For short journeys, such as a few hours by rail, a cabbage or lettuce tied in the basket will afford all the refreshment necessary. It is, of course, important, especially during the hot months, to let as much of the journey as possible be at night; and species from the higher levels of the hills should not be brought down at all during the hot weather.

In fact, it generally amounts to cruelty to keep such birds in the plains except in the cold weather, as many birds of this group are very intolerant of excessive heat; those from hot climates, on the other hand, bear cold very well as a rule, but all need protection during a winter voyage to Europe, under the conditions of close confinement and the bitter cold often experienced at sea.

Birds that have been long confined without the use of gravel should be allowed only a very little of this at first, or they will often kill themselves by unrestricted use of what is merely a mechanical digestive; many birds are, I am convinced, lost in this way, as natives never seem to realise that gravel is usually taken by seed-eating birds, and so do not give it.

Few people seem to take much interest in breeding pheasants, etc., in India; but any one who can rear chickens can easily do so, if it be remembered that the young of the wild game-birds need more raw green-meal and animal food than young fowls. A mixture of chopped raw vegetables, especially onions, hard-boiled egg, and stale bread-crumbs, forms an excellent food for chicks, and any insects that can be got are much appreciated, and greatly help in the rearing.